Gambling –
Winners and Losers

ISSUES FOR THE NINETIES

Volume 29

Editor

Craig Donnellan

Independence

Educational Publishers
Cambridge

First published by Independence
PO Box 295
Cambridge CB1 3XP

British Library Cataloguing in Publication Data
Gambling – Winners and Losers – (Issues for the Nineties Series)
I. Donnellan, Craig II. Series
306.4'82'0941

ISBN 1 872995 90 X

Printed in Great Britain
at Leicester Printers Ltd
Leicester, Great Britain

Typeset by
Claire Boyd

Cover
The illustration on the front cover is by
Anthony Haythornthwaite / Folio Collective.

CONTENTS

Introduction

Gambling – Winners and Losers is the twenty-ninth volume in the series: **Issues For The Nineties**. The aim of this series is to offer up-to-date information about important issues in our world.

Gambling – Winners and Losers examines the current debate about gambling. The information comes from a wide variety of sources and includes:

Government reports and statistics
Newspaper reports and features
Magazine articles and surveys
Literature from lobby groups
and charitable organisations.

It is hoped that, as you read about the many aspects of the issues explored in this book, you will critically evaluate the information presented. It is important that you decide whether you are being presented with facts or opinions. Does the writer give a biased or an unbiased report? If an opinion is being expressed, do you agree with the writer?

Gambling – Winners and Losers offers a useful starting-point for those who need convenient access to information about the many issues involved. However, it is only a starting-point. At the back of the book is a list of organisations which you may want to contact for further information.

*****

Spotlight on gambling

From the National Council for Social Concern

Who controls gambling?

The Government takes responsibility for controlling gambling. In 1960 casinos, bookmakers and bingo clubs were legalised in Great Britain.

Casinos
By July 1970, when the Gaming Act 1968 came into force, there were over 1,000 places for casino gambling. The 1968 Act had the effect of reducing this number. At present, there are only 120 licensed clubs in the UK.

In some games, like backgammon, members play against each other and all have an equal chance to win. Casinos make their real profits in games such as roulette and blackjack. Players stake their money against the 'house'.

Odds are in favour of the casino so it wins more money than it loses.

Bingo
Bingo clubs have proved popular for women with families and the elderly who value meeting friends as much as they enjoy the game. Several clubs can join together in common games which pay out a big jackpot. Total stake money was £600 million per year in the early 1990s. Some players go for as many as nine sessions a week.

One-arm bandits
Gaming machines include 'AWP' (amusement-with-prize) fruit machines as well as the larger-stake jackpot machines. AWPs are widely seen in pubs, railway-station cafes and amusement arcades. Jackpot machines are only permitted in registered and licensed clubs and institutes.

Machines can be addictive. People often feel close to a win and get hooked.

Betting
In the early 1990s there were over 12,000 betting shops in the UK. Besides horse-racing, there is gambling on greyhound races. Bets can be placed on everything from who will win the Grand National to whether it will snow on Christmas Day. A 7.75% tax is charged on each bet. Bookmakers say this is encouraging illegal betting shops. As much as £500 million a year may be wagered illegally to escape tax. In 1994 betting shops were encouraged to abandon their shabby image and were allowed to provide food and soft drinks for their customers.

The pools
The football pools are a type of 'pool betting'. The stakes of those taking part are pooled. Some money is deducted to cover expenses, tax and profits. What is left is shared amongst the winners.

Lotteries
National lotteries are common in many countries throughout the world and Britain's national lottery started in 1994. It raises money for 'good causes' and the arts. It is illegal to run public lotteries for commercial or private gain. A society that wants to run a public lottery must register with its local authority. If the turnover is likely to be over £10,000, the lottery must be registered with the Gaming Board. The Board also registers all local authority lotteries. Every lottery must have a specific use for the money raised and it can be spent only on this purpose.

Competitions
Prize competitions include 'Spot the Ball' contests and similar activities run by newspapers, TV programmes, and others. There is growing concern about so called 'skill' competitions which are easy to complete. A premium-rate telephone charge is made from which the organisers benefit.

● The above is an extract from *Spotlight on Gambling, Number 3,* produced by the National Council for Social Concern. See page 39 for address details.
© The National Council for Social Concern

UK Forum on young people and gambling

Working with the issues of young gamblers

One side of the coin

Why gamble?

Around 66% of adolescents and 94% of adults gamble. We like it because:

- It is fun
- It is easily available
- It provides entertainment
- It is sometimes possible to make money
- It is part of the culture of this country
- It is part of human nature to take risks
- It can seem like a magical world of fantasy
- Feelings of taking a chance can be very enjoyable

Who gets the money?

The gaming industry:

The Home Office have revised their rough estimates on turnover sharply upward for 1993/94:

Total gaming turnover approx £23 billion

Total spend approx £6 billion

The Government:

Customs & Excise figures 1994:

Betting duties	£849 million
Slot machines	£104 million
Other gambling	£161 million

Total betting & gaming £1,114 million

The punter:

Very occasionally a vast fortune is won from betting, the pools, at the casino, or weekly on the lottery. Smaller amounts are won every day by thousands of people from all types of gambling activity, although in many cases the amount won does not cover their outlay.

The other side of the coin

Is it harmful?

For most of us gambling is okay, but gambling can become addictive. Estimates vary, but more than 3% of adolescents and 6% of adults who gamble develop serious problems of dependency on gambling. A gambling dependency is very destructive.

Gambling dependency is often called the 'hidden addiction' because:

- There are no physical symptoms
- Gamblers can be very plausible and adept liars
- Money shortages and debts can easily be explained away
- Gamblers do not believe they have a problem, or they hide it
- Young gamblers often behave excessively in other ways.

Some of the more apparent symptoms that a problem gambler might display are:

- Cannot stop gambling whether winning or losing
- Winnings are put straight back into more gambling
- No limit is set on how much they will gamble at a time
- All financial resources go into gambling

Home economics

Average weekly household spending (selected items)

Beer/cider	£7.38
Take-away food	£5.13
Telephone	£4.87
Milk	£2.49
National Lottery	£2.10
Newspapers	£2.08
Bread	£1.80
Toiletries/soap	£1.69
Flowers/plants	£1.62
Potatoes	£1.15

Source: CSO

- They may form a relationship with a particular machine, betting venue, or gaming table
- They tend to gamble alone for long periods.

Hedging your bets

Is it legal?

The major gambling operations available in the UK are:

Off-course betting
On-course betting
Slot machines
Casinos
Football pools
Bingo
Lotteries

All gambling is regulated by law and current legislation is mostly contained in the Acts of 1976, 1963 and 1968. There is also the National Lottery Act of 1993.

Because gambling can be addictive and is recognised as having a potentially harmful effect if taken to excess, availability is generally restricted to adults aged 18 or over, or, with the pools and lotteries, aged 16 or over. The one exception to this rule is that of amusement with prizes machines (fruit machines) which have no legal minimum age restriction.

Recognising the anomaly of this, many inland amusement arcade owners follow a voluntary code of practice and ban those under 18 or under 16. The ban is less specific at seaside resorts where arcades are places of family entertainment and children are usually only excluded during school hours.

Should we gamble?

The opportunities to gamble are increasing and the urge to take risks is recognised as an essential part of our psychological make-up.

So gambling is an OK activity if like many other enjoyable aspects of life it is treated with respect and played in moderation.

What is good gambling?

Whenever you gamble it is wise to remember that:
- You are buying entertainment, not investing your money
- You are very unlikely to make money by gambling

- The gaming industry and Government are the real winners
- You should only gamble with money you can afford to lose
- Problems will arise if you become preoccupied with gambling
- In advance of playing you should set strict limits on how much you will gamble
- If you want to make a profit you should quit as soon as you are ahead
- Gambling should take up only a relatively small amount of your time and interest
- Gambling within your means is likely to be fun and exciting
- Gambling outside your means is likely to create problems for you and others
- You shouldn't gamble to escape from worries or pressures
- Gambling dependency is as damaging as other addictions
- The buzz-words are *gamble responsibly.*

Seeking help & information

The UK Forum on Young People and Gambling, PO Box 5, Chichester, West Sussex, PO19 3RB, Direct Line 01243 538635, is a national centre for information, advice, and practical help to organisations and individuals concerned with the issues of young people and gambling.

Gamblers Anonymous, PO Box 88, London SW10 0EU, Tel: 0181 384 3040, is a fellowship of men and women who have joined together to do something about their own gambling problem and to help other compulsive gamblers to do the same.

Gam-Anon, PO Box 88, London SW10 0EU, Tel: 0181 384 3040, is the 'sister' organisation to Gamblers Anonymous, and provides advice and support to the partners and parents of compulsive gamblers.

Gordon House Association, 186 Mackenzie Road, Beckenham, Kent BR3 4SF, Tel: 0181 778 3331, is a thirteen-bed unit with a national catchment area providing a therapeutic residential environment, counselling, and support for residents whilst at the hostel and after their planned return to the community.

Local area projects operate in a number of cities and towns in the UK. Contact information available from the UK Forum on 01243 538635.

Lottomania

Winning the National Lottery is everyone's dream but the reality of coping with the unexpected wealth can wreck your life. Sarah Scott investigates the downside of becoming an overnight millionaire.

The National Lottery has taken the country by storm and the draw now dominates the early part of most of our Saturday evenings. However, with the multi-million pound winnings and the frenzy has come a down side – there have been several incidents of broken friendships and family break-ups, some even leading to more serious problems like nervous-breakdowns.

The newspapers have been full of stories like the woman who accused her daughter of penny-pinching with her £1.3 million win. 'The Lottery has torn our family apart' claims the embittered mother who went on to allege that all she received of her daughter's winnings was a free pizza! Even last month's £20 million rollover jackpot winners have squabbled over the use of their winnings, and have also had their house ransacked.

Newspapers were even more outraged by the story of the two women who are being treated for 'lottomania'. Both deluded them-selves they had won a fortune – one accusing her building society of stealing two million pounds from her, the other convinced her family they were being persecuted by neighbours because of her new-found wealth!

Experts say that when you buy a lottery ticket, what you're paying for is the hope and the dream. The hope means that your one pound ticket buys you 15 minutes of nail-biting excitement, of really thinking that you could win. So what if the odds of being jackpot winners are millions to one against? It's just as likely to be you as anybody else and anyway, you're convinced that putting down Brad Pitt's vital statistics must be lucky.

The dream is all those drunken conversations down the pub when you discuss what you'd do with the money. In your fantasies you've already stared wearing Versace, bought your parents a new home and saved the whale.

Psychotherapist Anne Taylor, who deals with money problems, says there's nothing wrong with a bit of harmless fantasy. 'Those 15 minutes of hope can cheer up your week. Most people aren't disappointed when they don't win because it's they don't really expect to. It's probably worse when people do win because they have no experience to cope with their change in circumstances and it can be very stressful.'

Lottery organisers Camelot are aware that winning can bring its own problems and provide winners with free advice on everything from sound financial investment to how to deal with the long lost relatives that pop up from nowhere.

Anna, 29, is an office worker who won the equivalent of several million pounds from the German Lottery three years ago. But winning caused so many problems that she fled the country and now wishes she'd never won.

'I'd been doing the Lottery for years and thought nothing of it. I'd never known anyone to win anything big. So one week when I saw my numbers come up, I was overwhelmed. It was the best night of my life. I just sat up all night with my boyfriend Stefan thinking about how we'd spend the money. We'd been together two years and were planning to move in together so I naturally wanted to share it with him.

I kept a low profile and the only media attention I got was when the local newspaper came round. All my family knew, of course, and I planned to give them all a generous gift. Maybe I was naive but I didn't realise there'd be any problems.

When I went to work on Monday morning, things were already different. Several of the girls were cold-shouldering me because they were so jealous. I ended up quitting my job at the end of the month to think things through.

My sister rang out of the blue saying she was really upset that I hadn't been in touch since I'd won the Lottery. She said it was just typical that I got everything and asked what was I thinking of giving her? A million pounds maybe? Then she

Is the Lottery taking over your life?

1 Do you stay in on a Saturday night instead of going out because you need to hear the Lottery results?
2 Are you not going out anyway because too much of your money is going on the Lottery or instant scratch cards?
3 Do you feel really let down, even depressed, when you haven't won?

However, any of these symptoms don't necessarily mean you have a serious problem. It's perfectly normal to get very excited about the Lottery, even though you haven't got a hope in hell of winning! And droning on for hours about what you'd do with the winnings may make you boring but it doesn't necessarily mean you're deluded!

Also, remember that people do win and enjoy it. Camelot spokesperson Marriana Crawley says there have been 218 jackpot winners since the Lottery began and most of those who collect cheques go home very happy indeed.

started shouting at me and telling me to go to hell. She didn't speak to me at all after that.'

Before it all happened, I thought I was part of a loving family and a network of supportive friends. But I soon saw their true colours. My mother couldn't cope with the fact that I was no longer the poor little daughter. I wanted to give my parents a nice sum of money so that they could maybe go on a cruise and put some in the bank, but they wouldn't take it.

That was only the beginning. Cousins I hadn't seem since I was three started turning up on the doorstep. They'd come hundreds of miles to 'celebrate this family joy'. They were only there for the money so I was determined not to give them a penny, I'd rather give it all to charity.

The whole experience had destroyed my faith in human beings. People judged everything I did. When I started charity work and got a bit of publicity, one of my friends said sarcastically, 'You're going a long way for a secretary aren't you?' Sometimes I secretly wonder whether Stefhan has only stayed with me because of the money. There's no point in trying to find someone else though, people only want me for my money now.

I decided to move to Switzerland – no-one at home liked me for who I was any more. I live in a very wealthy area now where I just blend in with everyone else. I haven't seen my parents in 18 months. I'd definitely have been happier if it had never happened. I'm used to a good lifestyle now – I have an expensive car, a huge house and I'll never have to worry about money again. But it's at too great a cost.

Lisa, 27, works for a computing firm and participated in a syndicate with five colleagues. The agreement was that if any of the numbers won, the winnings would be split five ways.

'I never thought we'd win anything. We only did the Lottery for a laugh and enjoyed discussing how everyone arrived at their numbers and who came close to winning. We all talked about whether we'd quit work if we won – but none of us really believed it.

Whole lotto trouble

Counsellor Harry James says money is an emotional issue at the best of times. But when it's a lot of money, some people seem to lose all sense of proportion.

'I remember talking to one couple where the husband had inherited a huge sum of money, but their relationship was in real trouble. They had lost their identity and everything they'd been striving for. Jobs and earning money and so on give us a sense of who we are so when it's suddenly taken away there can be a great sense of confusion and even loss. The worst thing is that you're meant to be happy, so who's going to sympathise?'

The instant win scratch cards can bring problems too according to a spokesperson at Gamblers' Anonymous (phone: 0171-384-3040), the self help group for gambling addicts. 'Gambling addicts don't spend loads on the lottery, because they won't want to wait a week until they find out if they've won. They'll want the instant pay off. At £1 a time, the scratch cards seem cheap and low risk. It's easy to build up until you're spending all you have on them without thinking that you're taking a big risk. It's always, Oh just one more.'

When we won, I was away on holiday. It was a win of several thousand pounds but I only found out from someone in a different department. The rest of the syndicate didn't even bother to tell me. But the worst problem was that Hannah, the girl who'd picked the right numbers and actually paid for the ticket, said that she couldn't see why she should share it.

We were all stunned. Hannah took some time off work and suddenly became very hard to get hold of. I had her home number and eventually got to speak to her. She was really odd and kept saying that she didn't think it was fair to share the money. She said that if it had been a couple of million, there would have been plenty to go round, but with this

amount, there'd be practically nothing left after we'd divided it up.

Hannah became a different person overnight. I'm sure I wouldn't have reacted like that, but who knows, maybe I would. Money seems to change people. In the end one of the girls got a solicitor to threaten Hannah with court action if she didn't give in. The problem was that we didn't have anything in writing. We found afterwards we should have got a proper form. Eventually Hannah gave in with a lot of bad grace. Things have changed around here. We all got just under a thousand each. But it left a bad smell in the air. We don't play the Lottery any more and Hannah's leaving soon. Nobody likes her now. It was something that was meant to be fun, and she ruined it.'

Jennie, 26, found the lure of scratch cards irresistible. She started buying as soon as they came out in March and ended up spending £100 a week.

'I'd been playing the National Lottery every week. It was quite fun but it took ages to find out if you'd won. When the instant win cards came out, I went and bought five on the first day. I scratched them outside the shop and won ten pounds! So I bought ten more. Then I didn't win anything, so I lost five pounds, but I still felt happy. I'd never won anything in my life before.

I do two part-time jobs – cleaning and working in a local shop. – and earn about £250 a week. With this I was supposed to be paying off my credit card bills but instead I started spending all my spare cash on the scratch cards. I had to keep it quiet from my boyfriend Sean, because he knew the problems I'd had with my credit cards and had helped me sort my finances out. I knew I was doing wrong but I really thought that the odds were good. I had to be so secretive. I was afraid the newsagent would recognise me, so I began going to the newsagent on the other side of town. The most I ever bought in one go was 75 – not one of them was a winner. But even that didn't put me off.

One day I was outside the shop scratching when my friend Joanne came round the corner. I tried to hide them, but she forced it out of me and I told her everything. She warned me to get myself sorted out or I'd risk losing everything. Even then I didn't think I had a problem. I'd only been buying them for a couple of months and told Joanne I'd stop immediately, but I couldn't help myself and continued to buy them. Then I finally admitted to Joanne I had a problem and she put me in touch with a counselling group that helps people give up gambling.

I was amazed that there were so many girls like me. I thought gambling addicts were old men in casinos. The counsellor told me that as well as stopping the spending, I had to find out why I started in the first place. I realise now that the whole thing was an escape route. My life had been pretty miserable working so many hours. I didn't want to tell him that I was up to my limit on my credit cards again. He was so angry at first, but since I've been doing something about it, he's supported me.

I spent hundred of pounds and I have nothing to show for it. I feel very weak and stupid but when I started buying them, it was like it wasn't me any more. I've only slipped a couple of times since I got help. But even now, I see that sign outside a shop and can feel my fingers itching.'

© More!
2-15 August, 1995

Adolescent gambling

Case studies

Brian

Brian is 17 years old. He comes from a stable background but is now serving an eighteen-month prison sentence for burglary offences to fund his fruit machine addiction. He began playing fruit machines from a very early age and even at 9 years old he was stealing £10 a time from his parents to play the machines. Brian was always being suspended from school for bad behaviour and was eventually taken into voluntary care. His parents blame themselves, particularly because they knew that he had played on the machines from an early age and never tried to stop him. Brian says he plays the machines because he gets a buzz from the lights, music and possible jackpot. During an average playing session he will spend between £50 and £80. On one occasion he stole £140 and then spent it in the course of one afternoon. He claims he just cannot stop playing.

Dave

Dave is 19 years old and is serving a youth custody sentence for theft. He is the second eldest son in a family of five and there is no history of gambling in his family. As a child, he played fruit machines at the seaside with money given to him by his parents. His problem became evident at 16 years of age with constant arrests for stealing to play the machines. To stop him playing the machines, Dave's parents escorted him to and from his place of work until they thought he was out of the habit. As soon as they stopped meeting him his gambling started again and he was then taken to Gamblers Anonymous (GA) by his mother. Although he enjoyed GA, his gambling did not stop and on one occasion when his parents refused to lend Dave some money to gamble he took a tranquilliser overdose. The shock of the attempted suicide renewed his family's efforts to help him. He got a job in a cinema but the foyer housed a fruit machine, and he was soon stealing from the till to play it. He has now served a number of custodial sentences but the pattern is always the same after release. He gets his dole cheque, cashes it and then goes and spends it all in one go down at the arcade in about two hours.

Jeremy

Jeremy is 18 years old and is an only child. He has been gambling on fruit machines since childhood. No one knew he had a problem until he burgled his school and was caught. His parents noticed he had changed from a 'happy-go-lucky lad' to a 'bad-tempered monster' but did not know why. He had started to develop a problem and as a consequence began to steal small amounts of money from the home, to use dinner money to play the machines and to play truant from school in order to go to the arcade. Over the years he repeatedly stole from home, including various valuables and the television set. He is now serving a sentence for credit card fraud.

● The above is an extract from *Adolescent Gambling* from the Adolescence and Society Series – by Mark Griffiths, published by Routledge.

© Routledge

The National Lottery and scratch cards

From Gamblers Anonymous

What is GA's opinion about the Lottery and scratch cards?
GA does not have any opinion about the existence of any form of gambling.

Has there been any change in the numbers of calls to GA since the start of the Lottery?
Yes, over 17% increase in calls of all types, but not necessarily directly due to the Lottery or scratch cards.

Are the Lottery and scratch cards 'real' gambling like horse-racing or casinos?
They certainly are. In spite of the fact that you can buy these tickets in your local shop, they are still gambling. When you buy a ticket you have nothing for it except a receipt and a hope that you might win something by chance. Placing a bet is exactly the same.

GA is worried that the public are being misled into believing that the Lottery and scratch cards are just a bit of harmless fun for good causes. We are not spoilsports and have no opinion on the way the money is distributed, but it is gambling.

Is there a difference between the Lottery and scratch cards?
They are both gambling, but scratch cards are much more like being in a betting shop, and then placing bets and getting the results almost at once. The Lottery is more like the pools or betting on a football match.

Is doing the Lottery and scratch cards addictive?
We are not psychiatrists, and we have had them around for too little time to tell. However, a few years ago we did not think that anyone would get addicted to fruit machines, but fruit-machine gamblers now represent over a quarter of all members of GA.

GA provides help for compulsive gamblers. Is there a danger that there will be compulsive gamblers who do the Lottery and scratch cards?
It is still not understood exactly why some people become compulsive gamblers, but you cannot be a compulsive gambler without gambling, and doing the Lottery or scratch cards is gambling, so it seems reasonable to believe that in time there will be GA members who are addicted mainly to the Lottery or scratch cards.

Are men more likely to be compulsive gamblers than women?
GA at present has a majority of men, but there are women GA members. We don't know yet, but as the Lottery and scratch cards are available just as easily to both sexes then perhaps the number of women gamblers who become compulsive will increase.

What about young people doing the Lottery or scratch cards?
It is of course illegal to sell lottery tickets or scratch cards to anyone under age, but many children take an interest in these new forms of gambling, and probably do both. This is an early introduction to gambling, and as we said before is advertised as being just harmless fun. Even if the young person did not buy the ticket or card directly, it is still gambling, inviting him or her to share in the 'buzz' that may easily lead on to other forms of gambling.

Are there greater risks to the poor?
GA has no opinion about the effects of the Lottery or scratch cards on any group within society. The membership of GA is completely evenly spread across all ages, sexes, cultural and economic groups.

Is there any more information available?
We can supply copies of the following leaflets free of charge. Please send a stamped and addressed A4 envelope with your request.
The Wheel of Misfortune: What it's like to be a compulsive gambler and the affect of compulsive gambling on the family.
A Newcomer Asks: For anyone approaching Gamblers Anonymous for the first time.
Young Gamblers in Recovery: Helping to accept that you may have become compulsive, and 10 questions to ask yourself.

© Gamblers Anonymous
November, 1995

Gambling with their childhood

Scratch cards and fruit machines today – what will it be tomorrow? Angela Neustatter on the under-age addicts

Dan, 14, had no trouble buying five instant scratch cards in the week after they were introduced, and he's had no trouble since then. He says, with a broad grin and evident satisfaction, 'I won fifty quid the other day and seven times I've won a fiver.'

The fact that he's spent more than £150 altogether does not matter: 'It's worth it for the excitement and when you win it's a real high. I'd rather spend my pocket money on this than going out with my mates or computer games.'

Gary, 17, does not mind being disturbed at the fruit machine where he has been playing for the past two hours. He knows he can spend the rest of the day there if he likes. In fact he spends many days there. 'I'll say to my mate "What shall we do?" and then I know we'll go to the arcade. Sometimes I pretend I'm not going to, but we always do.'

And what is the attraction? Gary considers: 'When I'm wanting to go there's this uncomfortable restless feeling in my body that won't go away, then when you're on the machine and the lights and the hands are moving it changes and you feel in control. It's exciting because you have to act quickly and there's the atmosphere – being in an arcade is like being in a club.'

It is excitement at a high price. Gary says he can spend £50 ('easily') at a time. The money comes from a part-time job, money his mum gives him and sometimes he takes money from his mum's purse. His parents don't know where he goes, what he spends his money on, and he's not worried about it, saying he could give up at any time: 'It's just that I don't want to. I've always played machines.'

It is estimated that 1.5 million children under 18 play fruit machines every year, and, of these, 250,000 are under 10

Dan and Gary are not alone. It is estimated that 1.5 million children under 18 play fruit machines every year, and, of these, 250,000 are under 10. But it is the Lottery and the newer instant scratch cards which are being hailed as the greatest risk to children who may, all too easily, become addicted to the 'instant gratification' they offer. Luke Fitzherbert, author of a report for the Joseph Rowntree Foundation earlier this year, said he believed scratch cards should be banned until researchers discover the effect they have on children. He said: 'The Lottery could be fuelling a big problem of gambling addiction among Britain's youth. It may not manifest itself for some years but when it does it will be big.'

There are no hard figures on the numbers of children using instant scratch cards because legally they cannot buy them under 16. But a survey by Children's Express news agency, which sent out five reporters aged between 12 and 15, found that under-age children were able to buy cards at 62 per cent of the stores they visited and nobody really believes it will be made more difficult. Paul Bellringer, director of the UK Forum on Young People and Gambling, talks of instant scratch cards as 'paper fruit machines': 'We can assume as many children will use them as use fruit machines.'

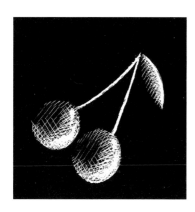

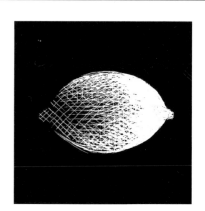

This is a far more worrying prophecy than many of us realise. Drugs, alcohol and smoking tend to be the focus of parental worries, and most of us are indulgent if we think our children are putting the odd coin in a fruit machine or illegally buying a scratch card. We tend not to make the connection that Dr Emmanuel Moran, a consultant psychiatrist and chairman of the National Council on Gambling, does when he points out that addiction, which is accepted as problematic in adults, does not suddenly happen on a 25th birthday. 'A four-year-old becomes a 12-year-old who becomes a 21-year-old and the compulsive behaviour grows.' That has certainly proved true with children who play fruit machines. Step inside an arcade and there, amidst the flashing lights, the whirring and shuddering of the machines, the dramatic chords which sound as you hit the buttons and wait, rapt, to see if the machine will stop with a flush of cherries, melons, or apples . . .there will almost certainly be youngsters well on the way to an addiction they cannot break – youngsters like Gary who begin by spending a bit of pocket money once in a while and who end up using every penny they can earn, beg and borrow, and who then turn to stealing to feed the habit.

More than 100,000 children annually, the vast majority boys, experience severe enough problems that they, or their parents, seek help, and Bellringer says: 'We anticipate at least as many problems with scratch card use and it could well be more.' People who work with gambling addicts point out that the most addictive pastimes are those in which the interval between staking a bet and hearing the result is shortest – with instant cards it can be just seconds. On top of that there is the 'heart-stop' effect – where you uncover two of the same number and have a moment of intense anticipation waiting to see if the third number will match.

Mark Griffiths, author of *Adolescent Gambling* (published by Routledge, £14.99), an impressively detailed look at the reasons young people may gamble, the pathological

gambler and ways of tackling addiction, believes that 11 per cent of all children will have severe gambling problems at some time in their adolescence. Most parents have no idea that their children gamble until money starts disappearing from the home.

We are the only country in Western Europe that permits children under 18 to gamble

---

Dave and Sue Jackson run Parents of Young Gamblers, an advice and support organisation with a seven-day-a-week helpline. They get 1,000 calls a year, the majority from middle-class families. Dave explains: 'Parents notice that possessions are missing, their child's trainers or Walkman have gone and they might then find out what is going on. But parents tend to think children will grow out of it. They come to us as a last resort and we wish they would come sooner. Addiction to fruit machines and scratch cards can lead to a lifetime of horses, casinos . . .the lot – and the crime, the prison sentences, the broken relationships that can go with compulsive gambling.'

The Jacksons run parent groups which help to plan a strategy for

dealing with the problem and organise therapy if necessary. Dave says: 'You have to find out if the child sees it as a problem. Most don't. If the child is sick and tired of lying and stealing, we can direct him to a meeting. Otherwise we tell parents to control all his money and leave nothing about. If the child gets into trouble then he must take the consequences – sometimes that does the trick. We advise parents to try to talk to children about what they are doing, and encourage them to find new activities.'

The UK Forum on Young People and Gambling has a range of very good leaflets telling parents what to look out for and what they can do, reminding them 'you are not the only family facing this problem'.

But our children could be better helped and protected if the Government would take the matter seriously. As it is, we are the only country in Western Europe that permits children under 18 to gamble. There is no age restriction for using arcade games and the Government has ignored calls by concerned groups to raise the age limit for instant scratch cards. Griffiths, who has seen as well as anyone the way children's lives may be wrecked by their addiction, says: 'By means of advertising and television coverage [of the Lottery] children are being introduced to the principles of gambling and will grow up to believe it is normal and socially acceptable.'

Organisations such as Children 2000 are aiming to get Lottery money used to help children who are already addicted to gambling, with funding for the UK Forum (which is at risk of closing due to a lack of resources) and to set up more than the one centre which now exists for children who need intensive care. But equally important is that parents recognise that this is a serious issue and that, as Dave Jackson says: 'We have to realise that there are a lot of people with vested interests in getting our kids hooked on gambling and we need to fight back.

We're not just talking about a harmless little flutter.'

© *The Guardian*
October, 1995

Teenagers who forget age limits for an instant

By Clare Gardner

Under-age schoolchildren at London's Parliament Hill School regularly stake at least half their weekly pocket money on the National Lottery, it was claimed yesterday.

Thirteen-year-olds at the all-girls' school in north-west London pass themselves off as 16-year-olds to shopkeepers if challenged about their age. None of them have been told to produce ID, they claim.

'They do ask my age at sweet shops but I just lie and they give it to me because they want the money,' said one 13-year-old who on average spends half of her £10 pocket money on the Lottery.

And would she consider herself addicted to the Lottery? 'No way Jose,' she said. 'It's just a bit of fun, isn't it?'

Another 13-year-old at the school said: 'I think it's great because you get the chance to win lots of money for just £1.' Some weeks she spends all of her £10 pocket money on the Lottery.

Getting her hands on the tickets is not a problem. 'I just ask shopkeepers and they let me buy them. I keep saying that my mum is outside the shop but she never is,' she said.

Others ask their parents to buy the tickets for them. For one girl, also 13, it is her father's frequent winning that convinces her that the Lottery is a profitable business. 'I buy a scratch card each week and my dad gets me a lottery ticket. I've never won but my dad always wins when he does it.'

Ever since it began, the Lottery has been a topic of conversation at the school although losing is something to keep quiet about, the girls said. 'If you win you talk about it, but if you don't, you shut up,' explained one girl.

It is a subject which divides the class. One 14-year-old girl from the same year as the others takes a firm stand against the Lottery. 'I don't bother wasting my time and money on it. My parents don't agree with it either. Our class is split into people who do and people who don't play it.'

Two shops within 200 yards of Parliament Hill School sell lottery tickets. Both are conscious of the need to prevent under-age sales.

Harish Patel, 28, a partner at Twin Peaks supermarket which sells lottery tickets and Instants said: 'If there is any doubt, we ask for proof that they are 16. We don't accept national insurance cards because there is no photo.' He said parents were the real problem. 'You get parents coming in with their kids and the kids scratch off the cards in the shop,' he said.

Anil Patel, 40, manager of Parliament Hill News, which only sells Lukcy Lotto cards, finds it necessary to challenge a couple of children a week. 'Ninety-nine per cent of the kids know exactly that they are not going to get served lottery tickets, cigarettes, or anything else like that in this shop.'

This may explain why most of the schoolchildren at the school tend to purchase their tickets on a Saturday.
© The Independent November, 1995

How to spot child gamblers

Parents were last night warned to be on the look-out for the tell-tale signs of teenage scratch card addicts.

Dr Mark Griffiths, author of *Adolescent Gambling*, gave the following guidelines for parents concerned about gambling:

1. Money missing from home – often the first indication of trouble.
2. A sudden drop in the standard of schoolwork, caused by the power of addiction.
3. Personality changes – children hooked on gambling may often appear sullen and moody, and constantly on the defensive.
4. Lack of care over hygiene and personal appearance – children can become so preoccupied with an addiction, they forget their basic routines.
5. Getting in late from school – children may skip getting the bus to spend money on gambling.
6. Missing homework.
7. Coming home hungry – dinner money may be spent on gambling.
8. Truancy could indicate money problems, drugs, or slot-machine gambling.

Dr Griffiths explained: 'These are the warning signs that could be a pointer to losing money through gambling on scratch cards or gaming machines. 'The big problem with gambling is that there are no physical signs. Unlike drugs or alcohol, it is not always easy for parents to spot trouble. They have to be on the look-out.'
© The Daily Mirror November, 1995

Young gambling

Guide for parents

Gambling in the UK

Gambling is an exciting form of entertainment that is popular with around 90% of the adult population and 66% of adolescents.

Opportunities to gamble are increasing: Betting shops can open 7 days a week from morning to late evening; there is horse-racing on Sundays; football pools are more widely available; slot machines are to be found all over the place; and lottery tickets can be bought at thousands of supermarkets, corner shops, post offices etc.

Age and the law

Slot machines
There are two types: fruit machines with a relatively small pay-out have no legal minimum age restriction but many operators follow a voluntary code to partly, or totally, exclude those under 16 or 18. Jackpot machines have a much bigger pay-out and are restricted to 18s and over by law.

Betting, on or off course
It is illegal to allow a bet to be placed by someone, or let anyone inside a betting shop, who is under 18. It is the betting-shop owner and not the under-age gambler who would be prosecuted if under 18s were allowed to place a bet.

Casino and bingo
It is illegal to be in, or to take part in gambling, at a casino under the age of 18, which is the same age for playing bingo. You must be a club member before you can gamble at either a casino or bingo hall.

Pools and the Lottery
It is illegal to take part in these activities until you are 16 years old and operators who allow under-age gambling are likely to lose their franchise.

Problem gambling

The different gambling environments are attractive to a range of people, with the amusement arcade being especially attractive to young people.

Most people who gamble keep control of what they are doing and remain 'social gamblers', but a significant number lose that control and become what is known as 'problem gamblers'. Unfortunately, as there are no physical symptoms, they are not always easy to spot. They either do not realise that they have a problem or they don't want other people to know they gamble too much.

Some signs to look for

Taken individually these signs may point to some other difficulty but the more of them that fit increases the chance that the problem is gambling:
- Gambler cannot keep away from activity
- Gambling seen as legitimate means of 'making money'
- Gambles alone for long periods
- Borrows often but doesn't pay back

- Steals money or valuables from home
- Has money difficulties and debts
- No apparent interests, pastimes or leisure pursuits
- Blind optimism, looks only at the here and now
- Creates rows at home as excuse to go out
- Truants from school or absents from work
- Has mood swings, irritability, restlessness
- Lacks interest in family and friends.

Why get over-involved?

Gambling is exciting and many people feel good about taking risks. It is not clearly understood why some people get addicted but three possible reasons that lead to problem gambling are:

Action: the thrill, or buzz, factor becomes addictive and the gambler needs to experience it again and again.

Escape: becoming involved in the fantasy world of gambling provides an escape from the problems and pressures of everyday life.

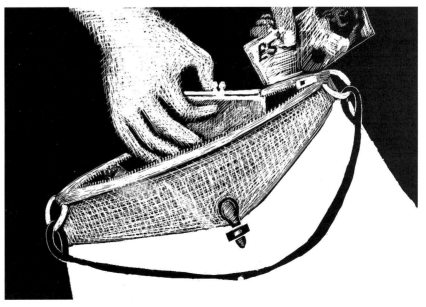

Beating the system: the gambler becomes absorbed in the technicalities of the gambling activity and unceasingly tries to beat it.

Consequences

Problem gambling ceases to be a social activity as the gambler begins to gamble alone for long periods. Relationships with family and friends begin to break down and the gambler often becomes isolated.

Even when not gambling time is spent thinking about it or acquiring money to gamble. It can become a 24-hour-a-day obsession.

The problem gambler will use up his/her resources first and then borrow with repeated promises to pay back. Many resort to stealing from home and some to stealing or committing other criminal acts outside the home.

The problem gambler is able to create very plausible and complex stories which they are then able to remember. They become expert liars to explain away the lack of money, the need to get more, and to account for the time spent gambling.

Truanting from school, missing college or staying away from work is also likely to occur. Over time this will add to the spiral of destructive behaviour and to the depression that many problem gamblers experience.

What can you do?

- Remember you are not the only family facing this problem.
- You may be able to help your child by talking the problem through but probably it is better if a skilled person outside the family is involved.
- Keep in mind that it is a serious matter and the gambler cannot 'just give it up'.
- Take a firm stand. Whilst it might feel easier to give in to their demands and to believe everything they say, this allows them to avoid facing up to the problem.
- Remember that they like to gamble and are getting something from the activity quite apart from money.
- Don't ever forget that they are good at lying; to themselves as well as to you.
- Let them know that you believe it is a problem even though they may not admit it.
- Encourage them all the time. They have to be motivated to change. This may not happen until they are faced with an acute crisis.
- Leave the responsibility for the gambling and its consequences with them. Help them face up to it and to work at overcoming the dependency.
- Do not condemn them as this is likely to be unhelpful and may drive them back to gambling. However, setting firm and fair boundaries to their behaviour is constructive.
- Despite what he or she has done let them know you still love them. Do this even if you have to make a 'tough love' decision such as asking them to leave home.
- Do not trust them with money until the dependency is broken. If they are agreeable it is a helpful strategy for a short period of time to manage their money for them.

Support for you

A problem gambler within the family causes turmoil and creates all sorts of feelings such as sadness, guilt, anger, bewilderment, helplessness and frustration.

Support for you from other family members is very important. Support outside the family from others who have had a similar experience may also help.

Support for the young gambler

Help and advice centres specifically for young problem gamblers are few and far between but there may be one near you.

Local youth counselling centres provide confidential counselling on a range of subjects which increasingly includes problem gambling.

Throughout the country there are branches of Gamblers Anonymous which are able to help young adults who can respond to the GA approach.

Where to find help

- UK Forum on Young People & Gambling, PO Box 5, Chichester, West Sussex PO19 3RB. Tel: 01243 538635. The national centre for information advice and practical help on the issues of young people and gambling. Working-hours advice line and 24-hour answerphone for young problem gamblers and any member of their family.
- Gam-Anon, PO Box 88, London SW10 0EU. Tel: 0171 3843040. Parallel organisation to Gamblers Anonymous providing support and understanding to the partners and families of compulsive gamblers. Separate weekly meetings at most branches of GA.
- Gamblers Anonymous, PO Box 88, London SW10 0EU. Tel: 0171 3843040. The national self-help group for compulsive gamblers. Weekly meetings at some 200 branches throughout the UK.
- Local area projects and counselling services operate in many towns throughout the UK. Check local directories or contact the UK Forum.

© *UK Forum on Young People and Gambling*

ID cards call for teenage gamblers

By John Rentoul, Political Correspondent

Tighter controls on arcade gambling machines were demanded yesterday by Gamblers Anonymous as MPs studied Home Office rules to restrict access to new machines offering up to £10 cash prizes.

The police should issue identity cards to 18-year-olds to enable arcade managers to enforce the rules, said Paul Bellringer, of Gamblers Anonymous and the UK Forum on Young People and Gambling.

He was giving evidence to the Commons Select Committee on Deregulation, which is looking at Home Office rules to 'fence off' the new machines within arcades when they are brought in later this year.

Mr Bellringer told MPs that in one region, the north-west, which includes the resort of Blackpool, four in 10 regular members, half under 25, have machine gambling problems where 10 years ago there were none. 'Almost all have developed the problem between the ages of 12 and 14,' he said. The evidence was that the enforcement of the existing voluntary code – barring under-16s – was 'often quite lax'.

David Evans, Tory MP for Welwyn Hatfield, asked: 'Don't you think there's another side to that coin – amusement arcades help keep young people off the streets when they might be beating up old ladies?'

But Terence Neville, of the Amusement Arcade Action Group, attacked arcades as 'seedy places'. Asked by Mr Evans if the idea gambling machines present a hazard was not just a 'fantasy', Mr Neville cited Home Office research which found that young people became addicted to gambling in later life; that there are correlations between child gambling, truancy and petty crime; and children are attracted to cash-prize machines.

> ### The police should issue identity cards to 18-year-olds to enable arcade managers to enforce the rules

John Sykes, Tory MP for Scarborough, questioned whether the Home Office order would not 'impose massive new regulations' which would damage the amusement industry.

He was not supported by John Bollom, President of the British Amusement Catering Trades Association (BACTA), which claims to represent 80 per cent of arcade operators. 'We see this new machine as an opportunity but accept that with cash prizes there have to be some restrictions,' he said.

Age limits for gambling

Age 18
- Gaming in casinos
- Gaming in licensed bingo clubs
- Betting

Age 16
- Lotteries
- Football pools

Separate legislation exists to take account of different forms of gambling. Lotteries and the football pools are seen as relatively soft forms of gambling with low stakes and long odds, where the participation of young people is unlikely to give cause for concern. The statutory age limit is therefore 16 in these cases.

Harder forms of gambling such as betting and gaming, where the risks to young people are greater, are treated with greater caution and therefore a statutory age limit of 18 exists.

There are no statutory age controls preventing young people from playing amusement-with-prizes machines (commonly known as fruit machines). However, the British Amusement Catering Trades Association (BACTA), which represents the great majority of amusement-arcade proprietors, has a code of practice including voluntary bans on children under the age of 16 years from inland arcades and on schoolchildren during school hours from seaside arcades. 'Jackpot' gaming machines, which may pay out up to £250, are only permitted in licensed and registered clubs to which under 18s have no (or restricted) access.

My guilty secret ...I'm hooked on the National Lottery!

Tara, 16, thought it was just a game, but now her gambling is out of control

My problem with gambling didn't develop until the National Lottery had been going for a while. Besides the fact I wasn't old enough to buy a ticket, I just wasn't interested in it at first.

However, when my sixteenth birthday came and I got some money from my relatives, I went on a spending spree with my best friend, Kelly. We had such a great time and I spent much more than I meant to, so I had no money left to buy a birthday present for my boyfriend, Billy. On the way home we passed a post office and Kelly suggested I buy a lottery ticket with my last bit of money; that way I might win enough to buy Billy a present. I guess I thought I had nothing to lose, so I agreed. We took ages deciding what numbers to choose. It was a good laugh and I didn't seriously expect to win.

And the winner is . . .

Two days later, on Saturday night, Kelly and I were at her house, all set to watch the draw on TV in case I won. We had a giggle sharing our fantasies about me becoming a millionaire overnight and living in the lap of luxury. Our eyes were glued to the set when, to our amazement, three of my numbers were drawn. I'd won £10! Later, I proudly collected the winnings and spent most of it on Billy's birthday present – all except for £2, which I had left over. I should have felt chuffed at winning and pocketed the change, but I didn't. Looking back, I wish I had.

With the £2 I had left I couldn't resist buying two more tickets. With one ticket I chose the same numbers as the week before (I figured if I was lucky with the numbers once, I might be lucky again) and with the other I picked a whole new set of numbers, using the birth dates of all my family.

The gambler

From that day on, I continued buying an average of two tickets a week, but I felt I had to use the first set of winning numbers every week, just in case they came up and I missed out on winning. But after a few weeks of not winning, buying just one or two tickets didn't seem nearly enough, so I started buying nine or ten tickets every week.

By now I was totally obsessed with the Lottery. I did try to stop for a couple of weeks, but I still watched the draw to see if any of my regular numbers were selected. Kelly kept trying to tell me what a slim chance I had of winning, but I didn't care.

Out of control

At this point, the Lottery is eating up all the money I make in my Saturday job. In fact, I even stole a couple of pounds out of my mum's purse so I'd have enough to buy a few more tickets. I felt terrible afterwards, but I couldn't bring myself to tell her. She has no idea and would be shocked to know just how many tickets I buy. So now I borrow money from my friends. Besides worrying about money, my friendship with Kelly isn't nearly as strong as it once was. She keeps telling me how stupid gambling is, and in a way I know she's right.

Sometimes I do win £10 or so, but instead of using it to pay people back, I spend it on more tickets and lose it all over again. Now I don't even wait for the Saturday draw – I quite often buy the 'Lottery Instants' cards during the week. I know this compulsion is ruining my life, but I can't seem to stop. If I can't afford to buy a ticket one week, I always buy an extra one the next. I know I should stop, but I can't. I don't know where to turn, and I'm scared that eventually I'll get found out.

Advice

Sure, gambling can seem mighty tempting, but it's bad news, simple as that. If Tara were to take a good look at the statistics, she'd realise that she has a greater chance of marrying Keanu than becoming a millionaire! So if you, like Tara, really want to see your money grow, do it the smart way – go to your local bank and put it into an interest-bearing account. Any other way is just plain foolish.

Tara's best bet to quit gambling is to go 'cold turkey' – and that includes not watching the Saturday night draw. Sure, it won't be easy, but the alternative – losing all her money as well as her friends' trust – is far worse.

Gamblers Anonymous (tel: 0171 384 3040) offers counselling and advice to anyone who has a problem with gambling, and everything you say will be kept strictly confidential.

© Just Seventeen
23 August, 1995

Scratch cards and lottery tickets

Ban on under-18s buying scratch cards and lottery tickets urged by Gaming Board

Alan Travis, Home Affairs Editor

Sales of National Lottery tickets and instant scratch cards should be banned to children under 18, the betting industry's official regulator, the Gaming Board, recommended yesterday.

The Board's annual report says the minimum age for playing the Lottery and particularly the instant scratch card game – which it describes as a 'harder form of gambling' – should be raised from 16 to bring it in line with the legal age for casino gambling, horse-race betting and bingo.

Sales of the Instants cards reached £38 million a week within a fortnight of their launch in March, more than matching the annual sales for the entire UK scratch card market.

The Gaming Board also calls for research into the possible link between the amount of compulsive gambling and the impact of the introduction of the National Lottery and Sunday horse-racing. It welcomes a Home Office decision to fund two projects and the establishment of a Chair of Gambling Studies at Salford University, funded by the casino industry.

The Board's report says it is concerned that the introduction of the National Lottery last November has already had a substantial impact on what has been regarded as the minimum acceptable levels of stake as well as the maximum levels of prizes in the industry. Overnight the National Lottery has established the £1 ticket as the minimum norm.

The Gaming Board says there is a real danger that 'a ratchet' effect will take place, with the gaming industry seeking to match or better the concessions given to the National Lottery.

The regulators describe the instant game as 'a short odds, quick pay-out, repetitive type of game, with an inevitable tendency for some to chase their losses by buying further tickets'.

Lady Littler, the Gaming Board chairwoman, yesterday pointed to press reports that some people were spending hundreds of pounds on scratch cards: 'The point about the instant cards is that there is a tremendous temptation to go on and on buying one. You are tempted if you have a small win to blow it on some more cards. If you do not have a small win you are tempted to go on and have another go.'

But Camelot, the National Lottery operator, defended the 16 minimum age limit for the scratch cards and the weekly draw: 'This is not about gambling but spending a couple of pounds on a flutter. It is the same age for the football pools,' said a Camelot spokeswoman. She added that genuine gamblers preferred games with shorter odds and an element of skill.

● An £18-million Lottery winner, Mukhtar Mohidin, aged 40, is to sue his wife Sayeeda, aged 33, to stop her getting her hands on his winnings. The former Blackburn factory worker who was the first rollover jackpot winner in December is said to be angry that his wife has given away too much money to her relatives. She has filed a counter High Court writ claiming that under the Married Women's Property Act the money is jointly owned.

© The Guardian July, 1995

The thrill is not the kill

Allan, 42, is a solicitor and a reformed compulsive gambler

My father gambled, my brother gambled, all my uncles and cousins gambled and I was just drawn into it. I started when I was 10 and stopped when I was 32. I gambled on horses, cards, dogs, casinos, anything. Whatever I had, I lost. When I gave up in 1986, I owed over £40,000.

I'd go into work in the morning, but the minute it came to one o'clock I was gone – down to the bookies, or the dog track or casino. I'd only go home when the money ran out. It affected my wife very badly. We had two young children. If our parents hadn't helped out we'd have starved. All I cared about was getting money to gamble with. I didn't care if there was food, if the children were clothed or if the bills were paid.

I'd love to have a flutter now, but I'm too frightened, even after 18 years, to go back to it. It's the compulsion, not the money that's important. I once walked out of a betting shop with two sacks of money and lost it in a couple of days. It's not about winning or losing. It's about being there.

© The Independent January, 1996

Gambling with the nation's health?

The social impact of the National Lottery needs to be researched

The initial enthusiasm that greeted the National Lottery is giving way to cynicism in the face of bad publicity. The controversy about the payment of almost £13m for the Churchill archives[1] was followed rapidly by the suicide of a man who had forgotten to buy his ticket;[2] criticism by the Public Accounts Committee of the £20m cost of distributing funds;[3] publication of unexpectedly high profits by Camelot (the Lottery's organiser)[4] and, finally, the evidence of the personal problems associated with large winnings and, especially, the much publicised disputes in a family that won £18m.[5] While these dramatic events have captured the headlines, there is also a growing recognition that a system that takes a net £50m each week from the public may have adverse effects on society.

If the Lottery widens inequalities of income it will have important implications for health, as shown by evidence of an association between inequality of income in industrialised countries and lower life expectancy.[6] Within the United Kingdom there is an enormous body of data on inequalities in health,[7] together with evidence that the health status of some age groups in the poorest areas has declined in recent years.[8] Many believe that the Lottery will widen inequalities, with even the *Economist* noting that lotteries tend to gather money from poor people to be spent on amusements for wealthy people.[9]

So what is the evidence? A recent report on the impact of the Lottery on society commissioned by the Joseph Rowntree Foundation seeks to provide it.[10] The first question is whether the Lottery is regressive in that it takes a disproportionate share from the poorest people. On this the report offers little help. It notes that the Lottery's regulatory body, OFLOT, is required to act on evidence of excessive participation by particular groups but also that no one has been given the job of collecting this information. Indeed, for the foreseeable future the only information will be that collected by Camelot – and that is commercially confidential.[11]

If the Lottery widens inequalities of income it will have important implications for health

---

The evidence so far about the Lottery's target population is largely indirect, such as the observation that children are particularly susceptible to sales of instant scratch cards and that 37% of children watch the National Lottery draw. There is much more evidence on the impact of lottery sales in the United States. This provides a rather complex picture. One study concluded that lotteries are 'somewhat' regressive but that the highest level of participation was among the middle income group.[12] A large household study in Oregon found that the most frequent purchasers were the middle income group, but it also found that poor people spend a substantially higher proportion of household income on lottery tickets than the middle class and that lack of education was the strongest predictor of purchase.[13] A time series analysis showed that lottery sales increase with increasing unemployment.[14] Lotteries can consume a high proportion of household income – 4.4% among heavy users in a study in New York.[15]

It is far from clear, however, that such results can be extrapolated to the United Kingdom. The creation of a gambling research unit, as urged by the report, seems necessary to fill this gap in our information. Such a unit should also not overlook the public health consequences of the Lottery. Specifically, it should consider the extent to which the Lottery is regressive, especially compared with other means of raising public funds, and it should examine the extent to which changes in disposable income affect consumption of other goods relevant to health – such as fruit and vegetables on the one hand and tobacco and alcohol on the other.

The second question is whether funds from the Lottery benefit poor people – for example, by increasing access to sports facilities – or whether they go disproportionately to rich people. On this the report is clearer. As well as the more glaring examples of expenditure that benefit the rich, such as the grant to the Royal Opera House,[16] there is also more systematic evidence of bias. Allocations from the Lottery fund, measured as both numbers of awards and their total value, increase from very low levels in the poorest tenth of electoral wards to high levels in the wealthiest. The report identifies many reasons for this, including the need to provide cofunding of capital and for recipients to cover subsequent revenue costs, both of which are easier for those who already have resources.

The component of lottery funds that supports charities is intended to redress this to some extent as the main beneficiaries are required to be disadvantaged groups and poor people. But these funds have been the last to be distributed and any support from the Lottery is unlikely to offset the loss from reduced charitable donations by the public with the shortfall estimated at £57m a year.[10]

Donations to medical charities fall

Other potential health consequences arising from the Lottery include the reduction in donations to medical charities and the additional social effects of the relaxation of controls on gambling. These were relaxed largely to protect existing gambling companies and now allow longer opening hours for betting shops and for the shops to look more attractive, advertising of football pools and a lower age limit at which people can play the pools.[10] This combination of measures has been associated with a reported increase of 17% in calls to Gamblers Anonymous. [17]

The sheer scale of expenditure on the National Lottery – over £100m a week, of which over £40m is spent on scratch cards – gives it the potential to be a major force for good or evil. There is an urgent need for detailed research on its redistributive effects and its impact on family expenditure. Anything that makes poor people in Britain even poorer, especially if they do not derive benefits in kind, becomes an important public health issue.

Martin McKee
Reader in public health medicine
Franco Sassi
Health Economist
Health Services Research Unit,
London School of Hygiene and
Tropical Medicine,
London WC1E 7HT

References
1   Thorncroft A. Lottery grant of £13m secures Churchill papers. *Financial Times* 1995 Apr 27:12
2   McKinnon A. Lottery loser killed himself for just £27. *Independent* 1995 June 9:3
3   Purnell S. MPs attack £20m bill to distribute lottery cash. *Daily Telegraph* 1995 June 9:3
4   Cull A. Pay and profits justified by success, says Camelot. *Guardian* 1995 June 7:3
5   Muir H. Lottery's £18m winners fight to save marriage. *Daily Telegraph* 1995 Jul 17:5
6   Wilkinson RS. National mortality rates: the impact of inequality. *Am J Public Health* 1992;82; 1082-4
7   Bezeval M, Judge K, Whitehead M. *Tackling inequalities in health*. London: King's Fund, 1995.
8   Phillimore P, Beattie A, Townsend P. Widening inequality of health in northern England 1981-91. *BMJ* 1994;308: 1125-8
9   Life's a gamble. *Economist* 1994 Nov 19:17
10 Fitzherbert L. *Winners and losers. The impact of the National Lottery*. York: Joseph Rowntree Foundation, 1995.
11 Kentsmith E, Thomas S. Luck had nothing to do with it – launching the UK's consumer brand. *Journal of the Market Research Society* 1995;37:127-41.
12 Weinstein D, Deitch I. *The impact of legalised gambling: the socioeconomic consequences of lotteries and off-track betting*. New York: Praeger, 1978.
13 Brown DJ, Kaddenburg DO, Browne BA. Socioeconomic status and playing the lotteries. *Sociology and Social Research* 1992;76:161-7
14 Mikesell JL. State lottery sales and economic activity. *National Tax Journal* 1994;47:165-71.
15 Devereux EC. *Gambling and the social structure*. New York:Amo, 1980.
16 Ellison M. Royal Opera's lottery grant sparks cash for 'tolls' row. *Guardian* 1995 Jul 21:3
17 Tresidder M. Mr Nice Guy won the lottery. *Guardian* 1995 Jun 10:27

© British Medical Journal (BMJ) August, 1995

Lotteryisms win instant acceptance

By Decca Aitkenhead

There will be little hope of forgetting it all for an instant when the next English dictionary editions are published. 'Lotteryisms' – new words and meanings derived from the National Lottery, such as 'scratch card', 'rollover', 'Oflot' and 'instant' – will all appear in the new volumes, enshrining the Lottery's impact on our national consciousness.

A scratch card, as defined by the new *Chambers English Dictionary*, due out in August, will be: 'A form of lottery card with a thin opaque film, which is scratched to reveal the allocated numbers printed beneath.' Collins and the Oxford English dictionaries will carry similar additions.

If new dictionary entries are the words that speak for their times, then lotteryisms suitably communicate the past year in Britain. Explaining the decision to include 'scratch card', the *Chambers* editor, Martin Mellor, said: 'These days dictionaries follow the lead of the general public. This is a word that is in common usage and it seems that it is here to stay. We try to reflect the true nature of language without being too politically correct about it.'

As well he might, having added 'politically correct' to the official English lexicon in the previous *Chambers* dictionary update last year. Other entries in 1994 included 'date rape', 'needle banks', 'car jacking' and 'ethnic cleansing'.

'Yuppie' and 'bonk' were quintessential eighties entries. Now 1995 will be recorded as the year of the rollover.

'It's quite right that formal institutions should recognise something that 30 million people play every week. The Lottery has become even more talked about than the weather – and in this country, that's saying something,' said a Camelot spokeswoman. 'We've got snow all over Britain – but what people are talking about is next week's rollover.'

For such a seemingly frivolous subject, lotteryisms are grimly literal. The Lottery is proving a serious affair – £5bn has been spent on tickets since its launch in November 1994, and next week's rollover jackpot will be an estimated £20m.

© The Independent December, 1995

Help is at hand

From Gamblers Anonymous

There are psychiatrists, psychologists, probation officers, social workers, prison staffs and others who are aware of the gambling problem and are doing what they can to help. More and more members of the statutory and voluntary caring agencies are now recommending those with a gambling problem to Gamblers Anonymous and Gam-Anon.

Incomparably the most successful source of help is Gamblers Anonymous and its sister organisation Gam-Anon which is for relatives of compulsive gamblers. These are fellowships rather than organisations and they were formed in the USA in 1957 and came to London in July 1964. Today there are over 150 GA groups in England, Ireland, Scotland and Wales, and nearly as many Gam-Anon groups.

Compulsive gamblers and their relatives, who all tend to hide from themselves, come face to face with themselves when at last they attend these meetings. Other peoples' therapies (personal accounts of their own experiences) tell them that, however much they felt alone, others have shared their suffering, and in giving their own therapies enable them to face themselves and their situation. They recognise that their lives are unmanageable, and that they have no control over gambling, either their own or their partner's. Yet they recognise that there is another way of living and thinking and if they give themselves to it they can find it.

Gamblers Anonymous

The methods of Gamblers Anonymous are simple. The programme of recovery was taken from Alcoholics Anonymous. The steps of recovery are read at weekly meetings, and the chairman, one of the members, invites each to speak of his own experiences. This is called his therapy. He describes something of his gambling days and of his better life now. As a new member listens he hears his own life story time and again. He gains self-recognition. The meeting is his mirror. He learns that he is sick. His compulsion may owe much to his being sinned against, but he alone is responsible for his future actions. He must not gamble again. In this atmosphere of understanding he can confess his misdeeds. He begins to tell the truth. This is the beginning of a new life. His wife must know everything. His creditors must be faced and a reasonable agreement be made with them, so that they will eventually all be paid. This is repentance, amendment of life, and forgiveness is implicit in it all.

From this time on, self-respect increases. He can meet people freely once again. He no longer starts at every knock at the door and can walk down any street and not be afraid no matter whom he should meet. In this stage members speak of new discoveries; of the fact that honesty pays, the joys of parenthood newly discovered or of taking pleasure in their work and family life. The understanding dawns that a pound is a pound, and that the bookmaker, the gaming club or the gambling machine is not going to get even one of them. One will speak of decorating a room at home, and another take pride in having a real hand in preparations for Christmas. They are painfully growing up.

Others who have been longer on the road may find the freshness of the new life fade and experience to the full the arduous nature of the climb to rehabilitation. The commitments of the past must be paid, and those of the present be met. A budget which includes all this is made and must be adhered to. Above all, no debts, however shameful, may be hidden, and the budget must be flexible enough to avoid the possibility of the pressure of a financial crisis. Such pressures from any source too easily becomes an excuse for renewed gambling. There is little to spare either for holidays, Christmas or birthdays.

This is a difficult and uphill road; impatient people who tend to escape into a dream world now have to deal with hard reality day after day, year after year. This requires honesty and humility.

Some members return a second time – even a third or fourth time – after intervals of months and sometimes years. Their problems have usually increased, and they are ready to face all that is involved in seeking a new life. Too often it is left too late, and their new resolution has to be tested behind prison doors.

Members are not referred to any other organisations. They help themselves and each other stop gambling and recover their lives. Still, some need more help than the fellowship can give because they have additional problems which block their recovery. These may seek the help of other agencies.

Some psychiatrists have attended meetings in an honorary capacity, but they do not take an active part. They have not led. They seek to understand the nature of the problem involved. Their opinion may be sought and individuals sometimes consult them privately.

There is a considerable failure rate for which there are several reasons. For instance, not all who come are ready to break with gambling. People arrive at Gamblers Anonymous because they have problems. Basically, that is what they want to get rid of. But to each one the essence of the message is that he must keep the troubles (his debts, or worse) and deal with them, and get rid of the gambling. He may find that instead of this he wanted someone to take away the troubles and leave him with the gambling. He does not want the path of recovery, at least this time.

Gam-Anon

An even smaller proportion of gamblers would succeed in rehabilitating themselves were it not for the sister organisation, Gam-Anon, to which members of their families, usually the wives, may belong.

They have needs of their own. It is impossible to live with a compulsive gambler, especially if you are dependent on him, and not become bitter, cynical and unloving. If their husbands are to succeed as they walk away from the past, the wives must be content to leave the past for the future also. Because of past experience, many find it difficult to believe the promises and to hope for their fulfillment. Still it is not unusual to hear one say that when she woke that day she realised that she was happy – and she had not experienced that for many years. The work of recovery is shared between man and wife. Single – or separated or divorced – gamblers find the way much harder.

The wife has to change the pattern of her relationship to her husband. Previously she has probably helped him financially by taking responsibility for his debts, borrowing from her family or by working herself, and giving him a home and food, even if he brought no money home. In addition, she would nag him and question him. She learns now to make him accept responsibility, and to encourage him in his new efforts, rather than blame him for their difficulties. In Gam-Anon she finds peace, courage and understanding.

But the struggle in both GA and Gam-Anon is worthwhile because it brings back self-respect and the respect of others. It provides peace of mind and a sense of being human again. It gives purpose and pleasure in ordinary relationships and responsibilities. It is beginning to live. It is healing. It is good.

There are established GA and Gam-Anon groups throughout England, Ireland, Scotland and Wales (and also the USA, Canada, Germany, Australia).

© Gamblers Anonymous

● The above is an extract from *Wheel of Misfortune*, available from Gamblers Anonymous. See page 39 for address details.

This present article is the result of the author's combination, with minor revisions, of his two leaflets, *Gamblers Anonymous* and *Wheel of Misfortune*. These were first published by 'Crucible' and 'Interface' respectively. The author has developed these themes further in *Quit Compulsive Gambling*, published by Thorsons.

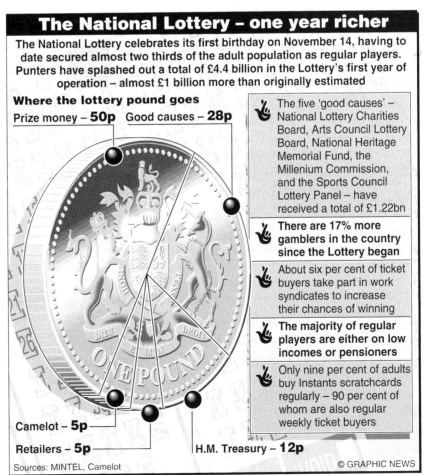

The National Lottery – one year richer

The National Lottery celebrates its first birthday on November 14, having to date secured almost two thirds of the adult population as regular players. Punters have splashed out a total of £4.4 billion in the Lottery's first year of operation – almost £1 billion more than originally estimated

Where the lottery pound goes

Prize money – **50p**   Good causes – **28p**

Camelot – **5p**

Retailers – **5p**

H.M. Treasury – **12p**

Sources: MINTEL, Camelot

The five 'good causes' – National Lottery Charities Board, Arts Council Lottery Board, National Heritage Memorial Fund, the Millenium Commission, and the Sports Council Lottery Panel – have received a total of £1.22bn

There are 17% more gamblers in the country since the Lottery began

About six per cent of ticket buyers take part in work syndicates to increase their chances of winning

The majority of regular players are either on low incomes or pensioners

Only nine per cent of adults buy Instants scratchcards regularly – 90 per cent of whom are also regular weekly ticket buyers

© GRAPHIC NEWS

Hope for compulsive gamblers

From Gordon House

Supportive group living

Gordon House Association's present residential provision is in two houses currently owned by Stonham Housing Association but run by the Gordon House Association. Up to 13 residents of either sex can be accommodated.

Occupying the time and energy that gambling used to take up is very important, so a great deal of emphasis is placed on residents developing other leisure interests both in and out of the house.

Residents have use of a pool table, TV, video recorder etc. in the house whilst all local and London-based leisure facilities are in reach.

Drying and washing facilities are available in the house as residents do their own laundry. They also clean their own rooms, cater for themselves (and care for Dylan, the house cat). There is a rota for the cleaning of communal areas.

One of the reasons the residents are expected to care for themselves is so that what help they need with social and survival skills can be identified and appropriate training given.

Not only do the staff offer support and help to those finding it hard not to gamble but so do the other residents as they experience similar stresses themselves. Being able to share and have peer-group support from others in the same situation as themselves is often what residents find the most helpful aspect of their stay.

Individual programme

Here at Gordon House each resident is allocated a key worker. They can also choose to have an outside counsellor. Over the period of their stay residents meet with their key workers, and counsellors if requested, on a regular basis.

Underpinning all the therapeutic work, key workers help residents set achievable goals that will help them resettle into a life not adversely affected by gambling. These goals are written down in a plan that also shows what action is needed, by whom, and by what target date. This plan is used as a contact between the resident and the house and the key worker ensures it is reviewed regularly.

Support by the key worker extends to help in resettlement, i.e. finding accommodation, applying to housing associations, etc. and that support continues even after a resident moves out. Ex-residents are encouraged to keep in contact and can return if they start to gamble again. We also operate a one-day-a-week Outreach and Drop In Centre a few streets away. Here anyone with a gambling problem can call in or phone, on a 'free-phone' number, for advice or help.

Every resident can also approach and talk to any staff member or the management committee thereby enabling them to draw on everyone's knowledge and skills.

Groupwork programme

Home-cooked food is enjoyed each Wednesday when residents take it in turn to cook a community meal. All staff and residents sit down together for this meal and talk about things in general.

Every resident after the meal, with help if necessary, writes down how their week has been. They have to be honest and say if they gambled or were tempted. They also write down other negative or good news matters that were significant to their week. Plans for the weekend are also noted as that can be a very vulnerable time for addicted gamblers.

Later everyone gathers in the lounge and residents talk about what they have written. They congratulate or confront each other on achievements or failures. Later the same evening a consultant psychotherapist comes in to lead a gambling-focused groupwork session. During this hour-long session any left-over issues or feelings from the earlier meeting are dealt with.

Project day-to-day business is discussed at a weekly house meeting. This meeting addresses the issues of living together and the management

of the house itself. Management committee members attend these meetings on a rota basis. Residents are expected to attend all meetings and join Gamblers Anonymous. Other meetings and talks are arranged on various subjects, e.g. relaxation, for those who wish to attend.

Clues to the compulsive gambler

Compulsive gamblers may be very competent at appearing plausible, blaming all their problems on factors they claim are beyond their control. They are not always easily identified and may not fit the criteria below – use this list as a starting-point only.
– Is he/she constantly in debt?
– Does he/she have few possessions?
– Does he/she have constant rows about money?
– Although broke, can it not be explained by an addiction to alcohol, drugs or any other costly habits?
– Does he/she seem to be an intelligent person with no obvious explanation for the mess his/her affairs are in?
– Is he/she evasive about how he/she spends his time?
– Has he/she got a record of shop-lifting, burglary, fraud, deception or theft from employers, family or friends?

91% of the population now regularly gamble. For most it remains a controlled form of entertainment. Those prone to becoming dependent on activities or interests may become dependent on gambling and many of them lose their home, their family, friends and possessions, ending up in debt without hope, self esteem or a useful future if not given help.

Do you think Gordon House would help you or someone you know?

We are able to take residents who refer themselves, referrals from probation officers, social workers, health workers, hostel or project workers – in fact anyone, providing the person being referred to agrees.

When someone makes a referral we send application forms to the applicant and the person making the referral. We also ask to see any relevant reports available about that person.

Subject to the written referral being appropriate and within our criteria we will offer a three-day (two-night) residential assessment. During those three days the potential resident will meet the other residents, will join staff and residents for a communal meal, take part in a group meeting and be interviewed by a project worker and one of our consultant psychotherapists. If at the end of the three days the individual wishes to come on a more permanent basis the staff and the residents discuss the matter. The individual will be given a decision, and hopefully a move-in date by the end of the following week.

An application form or more details of our work is available from:
Kevin Farrell-Roberts,
Director,
Gordon House Association,
186 Mackenzie Road,
Beckenham,
Kent BR3 4SF

The Gordon House Association is a registered charity (Number 274997). We need and welcome voluntary help, financial and practical contributions.

© Gordon House Association

Lottery jackpot curb is rejected

By George Jones, Political Editor

Demands by church leaders for a maximum limit on pay-outs from the National Lottery were rejected by Virginia Bottomley, the National Heritage Secretary, in the Commons last night.

She dismissed suggestions that huge prizes were bringing 'misery' to the winners or that the Lottery was unleashing a gambling epidemic that would disadvantage the poor and vulnerable.

Mrs Bottomley said large prizes increased sales – and in the weeks when the jackpot was rolled over, sales increased by up to 20 per cent.

Earlier this week church leaders claimed the Lottery was undermining the public culture and called for an end to scratch cards and a maximum jackpot of £1 million.

The Churches were supported by David Alton, Liberal Democrat MP for Liverpool Mossley Hill, who claimed the Lottery built up an element of 'hysteria and frenzy' with prizes as big as £17 million – and there had been a 17.5 per cent increase in calls to Gamblers Anonymous since the Lottery began.

But John Sykes, Conservative MP for Scarborough, dismissed criticism of the Lottery as 'sanctimonious claptrap'.

Jack Cunningham, Labour's National Heritage spokesman, attacked the profits made by Camelot, the Lottery operator, which he said were £1 million a week and rising.

Mrs Bottomley rejected Labour demands to curb Camelot's profits. She accused Labour of wanting to 'snuff out success' and punish profit.

But she promised to review the distribution of Lottery grants to ensure a better spread throughout the country. She also disclosed that some of the Lottery proceeds would go towards new 'millennium bursaries' to help talented young people.

David Mellor, the former National Heritage Secretary, warned the Chancellor not to increase the amount of tax it takes from the Lottery in next month's Budget, fuelling speculation that the Treasury was considering the Lottery as a potential source of additional revenue.

© The Telegraph plc
London, 1995

The British amusement industry

The facts – from BACTA, representing Britain's amusement machine industry

An £875 million contributor

During 1994, the British amusement machine industry will have contributed £875 million to the Exchequer – comprising £500 million in Corporation Tax, £275 million in VAT and £100 million in gaming Machine Licence Duty. This figure does not take account of the income tax contributions made by the 125,000 employed in the industry, the spending power of their salaries, and the input to regional economies through tourism and local taxation.

An industry of substance

The annual turnover for UK machines is approaching £11 billion, making it the largest element within the betting and gaming Sector.

A wide distribution

40% of fruit machines in Britain are sited in public houses, 18% in inland amusement centres, 15% in bingo halls, 15% in seaside arcades, 4% in single sites and 8% in other premises.

A business lifeline

The income derived from electronic leisure products plays a fundamental role in keeping thousands of organisations solvent throughout the country, including working men's clubs and motorway service stations. Machine income at some colleges and universities helps to fund important social facilities such as crèches. Electronic leisure earnings also play a fundamental part in the profitability of pubs, leisure centres, hotels, bowling and bingo clubs – in fact, almost everywhere leisure and entertainment are provided.

Paying out more than the pools

The most recent industry research

confirmed that AWPs and club jackpot machines paid out £7.2 billion in prizes to players. That is nearly 30 times more than the football pools and eight times as much as the first-year projections for the National Lottery. In terms of 'value-for-money entertainment', AWPs operate to percentage payouts of between 80-96% – three times as much as the football pools and almost twice as much as the National Lottery.

Internationally competitive

The international reputation and image of British manufacturers is unsurpassed. Machines to the value of £251 million were produced in the United Kingdom during 1994, contributing to a £76-million manufacturing surplus. The industry also organises the Amusement Trades International Exhibition which provides a platform for British exporters to market their products to a world audience. In 1994 a total of 23,561 buyers from 83 nations attended the annual event.

A major employer

125,000 people earn their livings from the amusement machine industry – equal to those employed by British Rail, and more than three times those working for McDonald's in the United Kingdom.

A breadth of entertainment

Some 522,000 amusement machines are sited in Britain, comprising 210,000 AWPs, 40,000 jackpot gaming, 75,000 pool tables, 75,000

video games, 35,000 jukeboxes, 30,000 pin tables, 25,000 kiddie rides, 20,000 SWPs and 12,000 minor stake AWPs.

A responsible industry

Home Office Report 101 stated: '. . . it does not appear that young people . . .are particularly at risk of becoming dependent upon the playing of fruit machines' (*Amusement Machines: Dependency and Delinquency*). Research undertaken by Croydon Council also showed that there was 'not . . .a problem of this kind (child players) in Croydon' (*Croydon Advertiser, 9/1994*). BACTA employs a Liaison Officer who has an ongoing dialogue with local authorities, Association members uphold a Code of Practice, and BACTA provides a free telephone helpline for individuals who experience problems with machines.

Supporting British charities

The BACTA Charitable Trust has a policy of supporting a wide range of domestic charities through short, medium and long-term fund-raising projects. The Association, which has distributed £600,000 to more than 250 local and national campaigns since 1983, adopted the Cancer Relief Macmillan Fund as its long-term project for the period 1994-97. Monies raised will fund the training of specialist Macmillan nurses who help people to 'Fight Cancer With More Than Medicine'.

Setting standards

A rigorous safety standard for the operation of kiddie rides has been set by the industry and recognised by the Health and Safety Executive. BACTA, through its IEC 335 initiative, is also leading the development of world-wide standards for the safety of amusement machines.

Target 2000

BACTA has set the following targets as it prepares for the new millennium.

- Increased prize levels for machines
- Permit payment for playing machines by means other than coins
- Permit off-machine advertising

The casino industry

Key facts and figures

- There are 119 licensed casinos in England, Scotland and Wales. 21 are in London.

- Two-thirds of all licensed casinos are ultimately owned by six listed public companies. No other company owns more than five casinos.

- All casinos are licensed as clubs to which only members and bona fide guests are permitted admission. No one under the age of 18 may game.

- Hours for gaming permitted by law are from 2 pm until 4 am including Sundays, except in Scotland where gaming begins at 7.30 pm on Sundays.

- Games permitted by law are Roulette, Black Jack, Dice and Punto Banco (Baccarat), Casino Stud Poker and Super Pan 9. The latter two were permitted from January 1995, the first variation since 1970.

- Total annual gaming attendance by club members and their guests in Great Britain (March 1994 to February 1995) was 10,991,751.

- The total drop (money exchanged for chips) in UK casinos in 1994 was £2.23 billion.

- Casinos' win or Gross Gaming Yield 1993-94 was £411 million, equivalent to 18% of the drop.

- Total direct taxation 1993-94 paid by the casino industry was £123 million. Total yield for the Government is £160 million, which is equivalent to 228% of the industry's profits after tax.

- The industry employs 11,000 people, 7,000 of whom are gaming staff. This is approximately equivalent to the total number of people employed by major companies such as Vauxhall Motors Ltd or Commercial Union Plc.

- Two-thirds of members of London casinos were from overseas or from non-British nationality. Net overseas receipts amount to £555 million. Income from this source is estimated at £120 million.

© *British Casino Association*

- Permit linked jackpots
- The introduction of a £5 coin
- The removal of 10p play machines from Gaming Machine Licence Duty
- Transfer responsibility for Gaming Machine Licence to the site
- Reduce the rate of Gaming Machine Licence Duty for sites with more than six machines
- Increase the maximum cash prize for prize bingo

- Give a right of appeal against the revocation of Section 27 certificates.

BACTA is the trade association for the amusement-machine industry in Great Britain. The Association represents the interests of 80% of the industry and has a membership of over 1,200.

- The above is from a leaflet produced by BACTA. See page 39 for address details.

© BACTA

Bingo and gaming

From the Bingo Association of Great Britain

A survey carried out by Gallup for the bingo industry showed that the great British public really do enjoy a flutter. Seven out of ten British adults had enjoyed a flutter in the past year. The indulgence might be as simple as joining in a works' sweepstake, or as deliberate as visiting a casino – but it's clear we like a bit of a gamble now and again.

But not all gambling is carried out for financial gain. The survey also showed that both playing cards with friends for money and visiting a bingo club were perceived as mainly social pursuits, with less than 10% of those questioned saying they took part in either of these for financial reasons. However, buying stocks and shares (which wouldn't normally be seen as gambling) and doing the pools were very much entered into with the aim of monetary gain.

The British perception of what constitutes 'hard' or 'soft' gambling is interesting. Buying a lottery ticket; taking part in a sweepstake; doing the pools, as well as going to a bingo club or playing cards with friends for money, were all described as 'harmless flutters'.

On the other hand, visiting a casino; placing a bet at the bookmakers; going horse-racing or visiting the dog track were all categorised as 'serious gambling' by around half the respondents. This is strange when you look at our gaming laws. Anyone over 18 can walk right in and place a bet at a bookmakers, racecourse or dog track – but the law says they need to fill in an application form and wait 24 hours before they can become a member of a licensed bingo club!

When asked to identify the gambling activities they had taken part in during the past year, going to a bingo club came second, with 11% of those questioned sitting down for a session at least once during the past twelve months. Half of these got their eyes down at least once a month, indicating that there are around 3 million regular bingo players.

Despite bingo still being a female-dominated pastime – nearly three-quarters of all participants in the past year were women – it's the minority of male bingo players who play most regularly. When these chaps were asked how often they had played in the past year, over a third (35%) said they got their eyes down every week; but only a little over a quarter (29%) of women said they played this often.

Less than half (48%) of those questioned saw fruit machines as being potentially the most addictive gambling activity. The one-armed bandit was pipped at this post by 'going horse-racing' (50%) and 'a bet at the bookmakers' (49%).

Notwithstanding the majority view, that dog and horse-racing are 'serious gambling', when Gallup asked whether people participated in these and other gambling activities for social reasons or financial gain, the vast majority were favoured for social reasons – or 'a mixture of the two'! Only buying and selling stocks and shares (92%) and doing the pools (67%) were done for financial gain.

So are we a nation of hardened gamblers? Certainly not ... we just like a sociable flutter!

Source: Gambling: Social Surveys (Gallup Poll) Ltd.
Gallup interviewed 967 adults over the age of 18 between 18-24 May 1994.

● The above is an extract from an information pack from the Bingo Association of Great Britain. See page 39 for address details.

© The Bingo Association of Great Britain

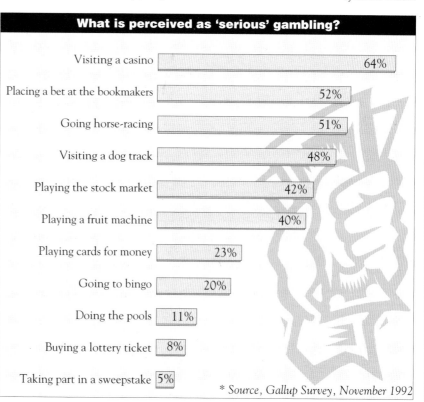

What is perceived as 'serious' gambling?

Activity	%
Visiting a casino	64%
Placing a bet at the bookmakers	52%
Going horse-racing	51%
Visiting a dog track	48%
Playing the stock market	42%
Playing a fruit machine	40%
Playing cards for money	23%
Going to bingo	20%
Doing the pools	11%
Buying a lottery ticket	8%
Taking part in a sweepstake	5%

* Source, Gallup Survey, November 1992

A guide to the National Lottery

From the Office of the National Lottery

Who's who?

The players

For the first time for more than 150 years, people in this country have their own National Lottery. This offers individuals aged 16 and over the chance to win prizes of several million pounds each week. On some forecasts it will eventually provide as much as £1.6 billion a year for the Good Causes.

The Office of the National Lottery

The National Lottery is regulated by the Director General of the National Lottery, Peter Davis, and his department the Office of the National Lottery (OFLOT). OFLOT is a non-ministerial government department. Its job is to ensure that the interests of players are protected, that the Lottery is run securely and fairly, and as much money as possible is raised for the Good Causes.

Camelot Group plc

Day-to-day operation of the National Lottery is carried out by Camelot Group plc. Camelot is responsible for all operational functions of the National Lottery including the sale of tickets, verifying winning tickets, paying prizes, dealing with players' enquiries, etc. The Director General awarded Camelot the licence to run the Lottery following a competitive application process in which Camelot committed to raising the most money for the Good Causes. The licence runs until 30 September 2001.

The game promoters

The National Lottery consists of several different games. Each game and its promoter is individually

licensed by the Director General. Games may be promoted by Camelot or by other companies and each game needs a licence from the Director General. Games promoted by other companies would also need a commercial agreement with Camelot.

Retailers

Tickets for National Lottery games are available across the country from newsagents, corner shops, supermarkets, post offices, petrol stations, etc. Main retailers sell the full range of National Lottery games and are linked directly to Camelot's computer centre allowing players' chosen numbers to be registered for draw games. They are also able to confirm winning tickets and pay most prizes. Some retailers sell only Instants scratch card games. They too are linked to Camelot's computer centre and can confirm winning Instants tickets and pay most Instants prizes. The network of retail outlets will increase from over 10,000 at launch to nearly 40,000 by the end of 1996.

Where does the money go?

The precise shares in the sales proceeds will vary from game to game

and from year to year, and according to how many tickets are sold; the more that are sold, the greater the percentage given to the Good Causes and the smaller the percentage kept by Camelot. As no one can know how many tickets will be sold each year, it is not possible to forecast accurately how the money will be shared out.

a) Prizes: The percentage payable as prizes varies from game to game, and the figure for each game is shown in the published Procedures for that game. Overall, Camelot must pay between 49.56% and 50.65% of all ticket-sales revenue as prizes each year (the higher percentages are generally given in the earlier years). Any shortfall goes to the Good Causes unless the Director General agrees exceptionally that some or all of the shortfall can be used to pay prizes in the following year. Unclaimed prizes also go to the Good Causes.

b) The Good Causes: The percentage payable to the five Good Causes varies from year to year and depends on how many tickets are sold. Of the first £3,500 million of ticket sales each year, between 25.31% and 27.27% goes to the Good Causes (the higher percentages are generally given in the later years). Of any additional ticket sales (in excess of £3,500 million each year), between 30.60% and 31.69% goes to the Good Causes.

c) Lottery Duty: Lottery Duty is fixed at 12% by the Finance Act.

d) Retailers: Retailers keep 5% as sales commission.

e) Camelot: After the above

payments have been made, the balance is retained by Camelot to cover its operating costs and profit. Of the first £3,500 million of ticket sales each year Camelot will keep between 6.07% and 7.03% (lower figures in later years). The company will keep 1.75% of any additional ticket sales (in excess of the first £3,500 million each year).

If, over the 7-year period of the licence, sales average £5,000 million per year, Camelot will keep about 5%. The figure could be much lower if sales are particularly successful; if sales regularly exceed £7,000 million per year Camelot's overall share would be about 4%. It could even fall lower if sales are higher. As Camelot's share falls, the Good Causes' share increases.

Note: Precise details of the amounts payable as prizes and to the Good Causes may be calculated by reference to the Licence granted under Section 5 of the National Lottery etc. Act 1993 (for details see 'The small print'). The formula for calculating the percentage payable to the Good Causes and as prizes includes adjustments for inflation and changes in Lottery Duty. Different percentages applied in the 5 months to 31/3/95. The notes in this leaflet are a simplified summary which do not take account of those factors.

Which Good Causes will receive Lottery money?

As specified in the National Lottery etc. Act 1993, funds for the Good Causes are shared equally by the following public bodies which will consider funding applications in their 5 different areas of responsibility:

a) The Arts Councils of England, Scotland, Wales and Northern Ireland;

b) The Sports Councils of England, Scotland, Wales and Northern Ireland;

c) The National Heritage Memorial Fund. This provides funds to save land, buildings, works of art etc. for the nation. The item must have some special local, regional or national importance to the heritage.

d) The National Lottery Charities Board. This is an organisation established to allocate National Lottery proceeds to independent charities and other institutions established for charitable purposes.

e) The Millennium Commission.

This is an organisation set up to distribute funds to projects marking the year 2000.

The small print

a) Legislation. The National Lottery etc. Act 1993 created the office of the Director General of the National Lottery. Under Section 5 of the Act, the Director General may license an organisation to run the National Lottery. Under Section 6 he may license organisations to promote individual games as part of the National Lottery. The Director General publishes an annual report on his activities.

b) Rights and obligations. Each National Lottery game has its own set of Game Rules and Procedures. These have to be approved by OFLOT and must define the legal relationship between players and game promoters.

c) Protection of players' Interests. A Player Code of Practice has been agreed with OFLOT. This defines the services and standards which Players can expect.

d) Advertising. There are strict regulations controlling the advertising of National Lottery games (especially where advertisements might attract children or encourage excessive playing). A National Lottery Advertising Code of Practice has been drawn up and agreed by OFLOT.

Copies of the Act and OFLOT's annual report may be purchased from HMSO. Copies of the Section 5 and Section 6 licences may be purchased from OFLOT. Copies of all other documents mentioned can be obtained free of charge by telephoning the National Lottery Line (0645 100 000). The Game Rules and Procedures and Player Code of Practice can also be inspected at every National Lottery retailer, who will also have available leaflets about how to play, information about winning numbers, how to claim prizes, how to form and run a group of players, and how much money has been distributed to the Good Causes. *© The Office of the National Lottery, 1995*

Profile of players

- 90% of all adults have played The National Lottery Game

- 50% of all adults have played Instants

- 65% of the adult population – 30 million people – play the Lottery regularly

- 15% of players play The National Lottery Game in a group or syndicate

- Average spend per week is just under £2 for The National Lottery Game

- Average spend per week is about £2 for Instants

- Players are evenly spread across all social groups, geographic regions and ages (16 and above)

- 50% of tickets for the National Lottery Game are purchased on Saturday

- Instants players buy throughout the week

- The above is an extract from *The National Lottery Fact File*, published by Camelot. See page 39 for address details.

© Camelot Group Plc

Winning projects rejoice for the people in need

Bess was gobsmacked and Laser was speechless yesterday as they came to terms with sharing the Lottery's charity jackpot.

Bess, the Benchill Ecumenical Service Scheme based on a large south Manchester council estate picked up £97,000; Laser, the Liverpool Accessible Sensory Environment Resource, received £150,000.

Representatives from both organisations were much too polite to mention Covent Garden or Sadler's Wells, preferring to rejoice diplomatically that people in need would be getting some of their money back.

'We're delighted,' said Sue Jenkins from Bess, formed by local Methodist, Anglican, and Roman Catholic churches. But there had been some anguished debate about whether money should be sought from such a source, particularly among the Methodists, who have a tradition of distaste for gambling.

No such qualms on Merseyside. 'You have to look at the Lottery objectively,' said Kevin Cowdall, of Laser. 'You have to treat it like any other fund-giving trust, admittedly the biggest in Europe. You have to look at the criteria which this time were geared towards poverty and grassroots organisations. We fitted the criteria.'

Bess was set up eight years ago to offer support, counselling and music and drama experiences to residents in an area of high unemployment and social deprivation. There are four support workers, two of whom work principally with young families.

The Lottery money will help develop a family support centre set up at the Methodist church a year

David Ward with two beneficiaries

ago. It is open five days a week providing a play group, mother and toddler group, clothing shop, and credit union.

'The residents of Benchill had no real voice and were not being heard,' said Ms Jenkins. 'They had very low self-esteem. The vision of Bess was to develop the skills and confidence of local people through music and drama.'

Laser was equally happy to take its chance with 15,000 other applicants.

'Every time you make an application to a fund, you are competing. It's a competition – a lottery,' said Mr Cowdall. 'Our application seems to have been what they were looking for.'

Mr Cowdall estimates that 95 per cent of Laser's potential client group will be Lottery players. He said he will look to City Challenge and other sources to fund the balance on an ambitious £850,000 scheme to convert the Owenite Hall of Science, in Liverpool, into a centre providing therapy, play, education, and stimulation for children with disabilities. At its heart will be a sensory stimulation room, hence the project's tongue-twisting title.

© *The Guardian*
October, 1995

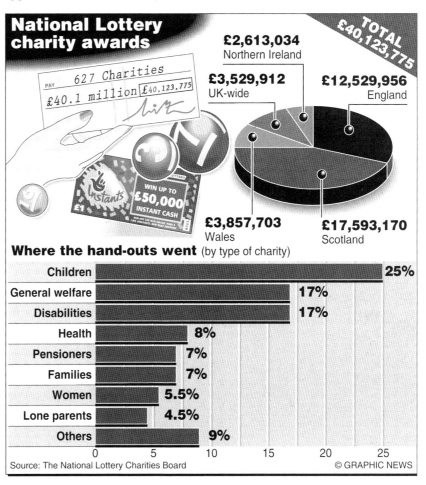

National Lottery charity awards

PAY 627 Charities £40.1 million £40,123,775

£2,613,034 Northern Ireland
£3,529,912 UK-wide
£12,529,956 England
£3,857,703 Wales
£17,593,170 Scotland

TOTAL £40,123,775

WIN UP TO £50,000 INSTANT CASH

Where the hand-outs went (by type of charity)

Children	25%
General welfare	17%
Disabilities	17%
Health	8%
Pensioners	7%
Families	7%
Women	5.5%
Lone parents	4.5%
Others	9%

Source: The National Lottery Charities Board
© GRAPHIC NEWS

It could be your good cause

From the Department of National Heritage

Raising money for good causes

In its first year the UK National Lottery raised more than £1.2 billion for the good causes.

This article describes some of the causes that have received Lottery grants and gives you pointers on how to apply for funds to make your scheme happen.

Who benefits?

By the end of the first year, over 2,500 grants have been made to projects, schemes and people who have applied for Lottery funding from the bodies distributing money for the five good causes:

– arts
– sport
– our heritage
– celebrating the Millennium
– charities and voluntary organisations

By 2001 around £9 billion is expected to have been raised for those good causes. Each month more than £100 million will be raised and divided equally between the five sectors.

In the first year by far the biggest number of awards was made to community-based projects – 78 per cent of awards were for £100,000 or less. Some big projects received grants too.

A wide range of projects and many different types of people have benefited from grants. The list includes:

– schools
– local theatres
– amateur musicians
– museums
– local conservation groups
– historic buildings
– community arts
– sports clubs
– woodlands
– the unemployed

– pensioners' groups
– disabled people
– caring charities, particularly those assisting the disadvantaged

This is a small sample – many different types of awards have been made.

How could it be me?

The money for good causes is there to reach every part of the UK, to benefit every section of the community.

Your scheme should be primarily for the public good, rather than private gain. You have to show that the day-to-day running costs of the project can be covered, although there can be exceptions, and you would need to discuss the project with the body you had approached for funds.

Most Lottery projects need some partnership funding. But you don't necessarily need money. It can be in kind in the form of, for example, gifts of land or buildings, or volunteers' time and effort.

The main aim of each of the bodies in charge of distribution is to give the maximum benefit to the public by supporting projects which will make an important and lasting difference to people's quality of life.

If you have a scheme, decide under which heading it falls, and apply to the distributor in charge of grants for that sector. Sometimes a scheme might seem to fall between, for example, sport and arts. Do not worry. The distributing bodies work together. They do not want projects to fall through the net and you'll be sent in the right direction.

People say it's difficult to apply – is that true?

Each distribution body gives applicants detailed guidelines on how to apply. It may seem hard at first sight but it is important to make sure

that grants go to the right people – and the distributing bodies are there to help.

Take heart, there are hundreds of success stories each month. Here are some of them:

Roald Dahl Children's Gallery, Aylesbury
'The National Lottery came along at just the right time; we had a great idea but only half the money we needed. Now our ideas can become reality. Without the Lottery we would still be trying to find the rest of the money.'
Colin Dawes, County Museums Officer, Buckinghamshire County Museum. **Grant of £254,500 was made by the National Heritage Memorial Fund.**

Penrhys Partnership Trust, Penrhys, Rhondda
'We will use the grant to convert two housing blocks on the Penrhys Estate for art and music workshops, recording studios and to provide other facilities for local people. I found the Arts Council for Wales efficient and friendly. They were rigorous but fair.'
Paul Rowson, Project Director of the Partnership. **Grant of £326,000 made by the Arts Council of Wales.**

Groundwork Foundation, England
'The grant will regenerate 21 urban waste sites into community open spaces for things like sports grounds, wildlife centres and cycle tracks. We thought our objectives were what the Millennium Commission was looking for. Clear information on key points like finance meant we were able to bring in partners at an early stage.'
Ken Davies, Groundwork Foundation. **Grant of £22,100,000 made by the Millennium Commission.**

Scope in North Wales
'We will be able to develop integrated employment opportunities for disabled and able-bodied adults in North Wales. We are glad that the Charities Board has identified themes for the coming 18 months; it helps with our planning process.'
Susan Ashton, Senior Corporate Fundraiser, Scope, for people with Cerebral Palsy.
Grant of £315,000 for a three-year funding programme was received from the National Lottery Charities Board.

Save the Cinema, Newton Stewart, Wigtownshire, SW Scotland
'Our community-led group has been battling to reopen the town's cinema for the last five years. There are no other entertainment facilities for young people in the Newton Stewart district.' We needed a theatre which could show films and stage live entertainment. We were particularly impressed by the Arts Council's advice. The outcome has united the community in its efforts to raise money for its part of the project.'
Iain Brown, Chairman, Save the Cinema Committee.
Grant of £340,000 made by the Scottish Arts Council.

Athletic Centre of Excellence, Antrim Stadium, Northern Ireland
'I am delighted with the speedy and efficient way in which our Lottery application was handled. From the outset, the Sports Council for Northern Ireland was helpful and co-operative. The procedure was straightforward and the information clear.'
Philip Lucas, Antrim Borough Council.
Grant of £35,750 for athletic equipment made by the Sports Council for Northern Ireland.

Lottery projects are the result of the vision of thousands of ordinary people around the UK. They often reflect collaboration between schools, community groups, sports clubs, charities, local authorities, local businesses . . . the list is endless.

They represent what people want to see in their area. That is important to remember – because it is people like you who have to come forward with the ideas.

Where do I go next?

If you think a project could be eligible for Lottery funding you should contact the distributing body that seems most likely to help. And remember, if your project does cut across boundaries that does not rule it out.

The distributing body you approach will send you an application form and other helpful guidance. The important thing is to help you get it right.

Who watches over the Lottery?

The Office of the National Lottery (OFLOT) is headed by the Director General. He ensures that the National Lottery is run with due propriety; the interests of players are protected; and, subject to the above, the maximum amount possible is raised for good causes. He does not supervise the distribution of Lottery money to the good causes. OFLOT selected Camelot Group plc to run the Lottery from eight applicants and makes sure that Camelot pays over the money due to the good causes.

World-wide lottery facts

The UK National Lottery

- One of the most efficient in the world
- Already largest lottery in the world
- Largest ever on-line lottery launch
- Largest amount of money raised since start-up – £1.75 billion in the first year for good causes and Government

- There are 165 lotteries world-wide

- World-wide lottery sales (1994) 61.5 billion

- Oldest existing lottery in Europe – The Netherlands – developed in 1726

- Spain has had a lottery since 1763

- Largest ever on-line lottery jackpot world-wide was California in 1991 ($118.8 million) and was shared between several winners with the same numbers.

- The above is an extract from *The National Lottery Fact File*, published by Camelot Group Plc. See page 39 for address details.

Lottery refuses 9 in 10 charities

Call for needy to have larger share of take

By David Brindle on the first awards

Almost nine in 10 charities that have sought National Lottery funding will be refused, the Lottery charities board said yesterday as it announced its first grants totalling £40 million.

The warning prompted calls for the board to be given a larger share of the Lottery's proceeds by cutting the Treasury's take, squeezing the other 'good cause' boards, or reducing the profits taken by Camelot, the game's operator.

Stuart Etherington, chief executive of the National Council for Voluntary Organisations, said: 'The charities board has turned the tide and demonstrated that the Lottery can help good charities very effectively. What the Government should do is look again at the proportion of money that goes to the board – and increase it.'

David Sieff, the board's chairman, said it was up to ministers to decide if more cash should go to charities. But he added: 'I certainly know how to spend it.'

Controversy continued to dog the board as it announced that the £40 million would be split among 627 groups – fewer than 14 per cent of the 4,500 applications so far decided upon. The success rate is expected to be even lower among the 10,800 remaining bids for cash under the board's first programme, aimed at relieving poverty and disadvantage. After advance criticism of grants going to groups helping refugees and other 'politically correct' causes, the board went out of its way to stress the breadth of its awards.

Timothy Hornsby, the board's chief executive, said: 'Less than 1 per cent go to refugees – and they need it. Less than 3 per cent go to charities dealing with drug and alcohol addiction – and they need it.

About 6 per cent go to ethnic minority groups – and they need it.'

About a quarter of grants were going to groups working with children, and household names among recipients included Citizen's Advice Bureaux (£1.9 million), the Royal National Institute for the Blind (£188,500), and Scope, formerly the Spastics Society (£315,000).

Some commentators had dwelled on a grant of £91,000 to the London-based Eritrean Advice and Information Centre, Mr Hornsby said. 'So much play has been made about one refugee group, but it's a jolly good scheme.'

About 44 per cent of yesterday's grants money is going to groups in Scotland. The board says that this is because its Scottish arm has made faster progress in assessing bids and that further awards over the next two months – the first programme is worth a total £162 million – will favour England.

The board has purposely concentrated on helping smaller, community-based groups, with almost half of yesterday's grants going to organisations with annual income of less than £20,000.

Typical recipients include the 19th Swindon Scout group (£1,480 for a minibus and equipment); the Hull Council of Disabled People (£59,000 for a transport scheme); and the Dundee Cyrenians Night Shelter (£39,000 for a new hostel for homeless people).

Some charity experts are calling on the charities board to cut the average size of its grants and spread its limited funds further. There are concerns, too, about the impact on smaller groups of a large, one-off injection of cash – although the £64,000 mean average award yesterday disguises the fact half of all awards are less than £50,000. The board says it vets applications to ensure they would not be destabilised and be able to continue smoothly in future.

The board receives 5.6 per cent of Lottery proceeds – as do the heritage, millennium, sports and arts boards. The Treasury keeps 12 per cent, ticket agents receive 5 per cent, and Camelot takes 5 per cent in costs and profit. Lottery winnings account for 50 per cent. © *The Guardian* October, 1995

A nation of winners

The Good Causes

The National Lottery was set up to raise funds for the five Good Causes chosen by Parliament. Indeed, the Lottery should provide the largest injection of new money into these areas ever seen in the UK.

Our role as operator is to maximise that funding. Our bid was designed to achieve just that. We committed ourselves to the lowest bid, in terms of the percentage we keep to run the business, which will enable us to give an estimated £9 billion to The National Lottery Distribution Fund for distribution to the Good Causes over the seven years.

We handed over the first cheque to The National Lottery Distribution Fund on Tuesday 22 November 1994. It totalled £12,659,380.83.

By the end of March we had handed over a further 18 cheques making an overall total of £317 million. We had more than exceeded our expectations with an additional £90 million, or 40% more than we forecast, being raised in our first financial year. By mid June this year over £640 million had been transferred to The National Lottery Distribution Fund.

Camelot is not responsible for the allocation of funds. These difficult decisions rest with the distributing bodies: The Arts Councils, The Sports Councils, The National Lottery Charities Board, The National Heritage Memorial Fund and The Millennium Commission.

By 31 March, the first funding announcements had been made and since then a stream of others have followed.

Sports grants have been made to projects such as a community sub-aqua club in Enniskillen. For years the club had wanted to purchase a new diving boat but could not find the money. Their Lottery grant will allow them to set up a community rescue service for the whole of County Fermanagh.

Additional funding for the arts is allowing youth bands to buy new instruments, dance groups to perform in appropriate surroundings and in the case of the Cardiff Old Library, which had £2 million Lottery funding, to bring together some of the artistic talent of Wales under one roof.

Projects benefiting from The Heritage Lottery Fund include St Lawrence's Church, South Walsham, Norfolk, which can now complete restoration work and convert its garden into a community arts and training centre, and the Eyam Museum near Sheffield, which is going to extend and improve exhibition displays with its new funding.

The National Lottery Charities Board opened for applications in May and within five weeks had sent out 18,000 application packs. It aims to support charitable and voluntary groups of all kinds and sizes throughout the UK and will announce its first grants in October.

The Millennium Commission is currently considering applications for funding capital projects and will be making initial funding announcements in August. It announced a first round short-list of 83 projects for further consideration on 15 June this year, all of which are competing for the first £350 million of funding.

Projects up and down the UK are taking on a new life as a direct result of proceeds form the Lottery. As they do so, communities large and small will experience for themselves the lasting benefits of the National Lottery. As operators, our objective at Camelot is to continue to run an efficient and successful lottery so that these benefits can be as great and as widespread as possible throughout the nation.

● The above is an extract from Camelot's *Annual Report and Accounts 1995*.   © *Camelot*

Allocation of funds

- Camelot is not responsible for the distribution of funds to the Good Causes

- The five Good Causes were chosen by Parliament: Arts, Sport, Heritage, Charities and the Millennium

- Eleven distributing bodies make decisions on the specific allocation of funds
    - The Arts Councils of England, Wales Northern Ireland and Scotland
    - The Sports Councils of England Wales, Northern Ireland and Scotland
    - The National Lottery Charities Board
    - The National Heritage Memorial Fund
    - The Millennium Commission

● The above is an extract from *The National Lottery Fact File*, published by Camelot. See page 39 for address details.

© *Camelot*

Council of Churches for Britain and Ireland

At the Churches Representatives Meeting 20th–22nd November, the Council of Churches for Britain and Ireland accepted the statement of concern about the National Lottery prepared by a meeting of Social Responsibility Representatives last month.

1. We wish to affirm the public culture which has been of considerable benefit to our society. In this, money from taxation, charities working at national and local levels, central and local government have co-operated to sustain the common good.

2. We are deeply concerned that the National Lottery is undermining the public culture which has served us well. We therefore identify below some of our concerns about the way the National Lottery is adversely affecting our society.

3. We acknowledge, however, that lotteries are a pervasive feature of European life, and in many instances provide a marginal, though significant, enhancement of public amenity.

4. All the Churches recognise that the National Lottery in the UK has provoked among their members a wide variety of opinion. In addition, the National Lottery confronts the Churches with certain ethical dilemmas.

5. Our concerns about the National Lottery are the following:

5.1 One of the achievements of Government legislation in the 20th century has been the regulation of gambling. The National Lottery threatens recklessly to dismantle these regulations.

5.2 The National Lottery's huge advertising budget, coupled with publicity in the media, have created a considerable likelihood of gambling harm, with little prospect of public benefit.

– The ready access to instant games, which are believed to be compulsive in character, illustrates the gambling harm.

– The relatively small amount of money which will flow each year to charities from the Lottery is seen when it is compared with other sources of voluntary giving and public expenditure.

– Charity Board allocations, £1bn
– Total charitable giving, £10bn
– Social Security expenditure, £70bn
– Total public expenditure, £300bn

5.3 Our widespread experience with charities and local government is that the overall effect of the Lottery is to reduce public expenditure rather than enhance public amenity.

5.4 The Lottery attracts expenditure from all sectors of society more or less evenly and therefore disproportionately from the poorest.

5.5 Our clear perception is that many vulnerable and desperate people are being induced to spend money on the Lottery that they cannot afford.

6. We therefore call for authoritative and independent research on all aspects of the Lottery; in particular we wish Parliament urgently to revive the recommendation of the 1978 Royal Commission that a Gambling Research Council be established.

7. Until the research is available, we believe the DNH and OFLOT should give serious consideration to the following interim changes in the regulations of the National Lottery.

7.1 No more licences for Instant Games to be issued.

7.2 The minimum age for playing the Lottery should be raised to 18 years.

7.3 The size of the jackpot prizes should be limited.

8. The most effective way of helping charities is by direct giving.

© *The Council of Churches for Britain and Ireland November, 1995*

Nation of gamblers

More than 70% of adults now play the National Lottery. Each household spends on average £2.05 per week – well under half the amount spent on cigarettes. Around one in five adults also buys 'Instants' scratchcards

All figures adjusted to 1994-95 prices

£m	Lotteries	Casinos	Bingo
1986/87	32	2,382	816
1987/88	31	2,437	886
1988/89	28	2,296	789
1989/90	29	2,329	765
1990/91	31	2,178	746
1991/92	60	2,063	771
1992/93	49	2,154	822
1993/94	44	2,291	811
1994/95	3,639	2,461	–

Source: CSO   © GRAPHIC NEWS

Churches attack big-win Lottery but take the cash

**By Dan Conaghan,
Arts Correspondent**

Church leaders condemned the National Lottery yesterday as 'undermining the public culture' and called for radical changes, including an end to scratch cards, a maximum jackpot of £1 million and a minimum playing age of 18. The Rt Rev David Sheppard, the Anglican Bishop of Liverpool, led senior officials from the Roman Catholic Methodist, and Scottish Churches in calling for the changes, but admitted the Churches faced 'ethical dilemmas' in applying for Lottery funds themselves.

Churches around the country have already received more than £1 million of Lottery money and there are no fewer than 267 applications for grants of £19 million, awaiting approval from the Heritage Lottery Fund.

Despite this paradox, the Council of Churches for Britain and Ireland, meeting in London, said it was 'deeply concerned' about the Lottery, and that it provided only a 'marginal' enhancement of public amenity.

Bishop Sheppard said the Church of England had applied for Lottery funding to ensure its buildings were maintained properly, but said it would never do so to finance its pastoral work. 'It is a great dilemma,' he said.

Nicholas Coote, representing the Roman Catholic Church, added that it did 'not see obstacles to particular Churches and dioceses to make applications'. He said: 'We are not going to cut off our nose to spite our face.'

The Church of Scotland said it would apply for funding only if the Government reduced grants to fund heritage

Although their joint statement admitted there were dilemmas about such funding, it was clear that the poor were disadvantaged by the Lottery. It said: 'Our clear perception is that many vulnerable and desperate people are being induced to spend money on the Lottery that they cannot afford.'

The Lottery's huge advertising budget had created 'a considerable likelihood of gambling harm, with little prospect of public benefit', the council said. 'The National Lottery threatens recklessly to dismantle [gambling] regulations.'

Bishop Sheppard said: 'We feel that many of the people who are most vulnerable in our society, who can least afford it, are being sucked into going for these big prizes week after week.

'They think there is going to be some very big win that is going to change their lives. That is a world of fantasy that does not help people.'

The declaration was backed by representatives of more than a dozen church groups, including Baptists, the United Reformed Church, the Free Church and the Quakers.

All the Churches believed there had been a very good partnership between local authorities which gave out grants and the public who made donations to charity.

Last month the Heritage Lottery Fund awarded grants totalling more than £1 million to 18 Anglican, Roman Catholic and United Reformed Churches

This had now been put at risk. Increasingly, churches reported instances of local groups being told by town halls to apply to the Lottery for funding.

Last month the Heritage Lottery Fund awarded grants totalling more than £1 million to 18 Anglican, Roman Catholic and United Reformed churches. The 267 applications pending are mainly for the restoration of ecclesiastical buildings.

It has also been suggested that the City of London's 37 Anglican churches, in need of £23 million for repairs and upkeep over the next 25 years, might apply for Lottery funds.

Earlier this year the Methodist Church voted against applying for Lottery funds for the maintenance of its church buildings or for personnel. But it agreed that 'in exceptional circumstances' a Methodist project, dedicated to work with the poor, might apply to the National Lottery Charities Board.

The Charities Board said yesterday it had no particular policy on applications from church charities, which were welcome to apply.

Among the 627 grants it announced on Monday is one for £58,000 for the Catholic Children's Society, based in Westminster, and another for £67,000 destined for Churches Action for the Homeless.

The Church of Scotland has been one of the most hostile towards the Lottery. Earlier this year its General Assembly decided it would be 'inappropriate' to apply for Millennium Fund money for a celebration of Christ's birth.

The Church also refused to apply for Lottery money for its 1,200 buildings.

Where £40 million hand-out is going

Controversy continues to dog list of charities that will receive Lottery cash

The National Lottery Charities Board vigorously defended its choice of recipients who will share £40 million in its first grants yesterday, saying it had 'met its objectives and kept its promises'.

Controversy dogged the announcement of the 627 grants. The Royal National Institute for the Blind said the £188,000 it received should be seen against an estimated £500,000 loss in donations that it blames on the Lottery.

David Mellor MP, a former Heritage Secretary, said the board was a 'creaky old tub' and grants to small community projects were 'piled full of some of the usual suspects of politically correct vehicles'.

David Sieff, the board's chairman, said the claim was nonsense: 'I would be very interested if Mr Mellor would like to contact us to find out what we are doing instead of just commenting on the sidelines.'

The board also fielded criticism of grants to projects for refugees, drug addicts and alcoholics; only one per cent of grants had gone to refugees and three per cent to projects helping addicts.

Among the well-known recipients, 13 Citizens' Advice Bureaux shared £1.9 million, Cancer Research Campaign received £282,000 and the Royal National Institute for Deaf People £195,000.

The response from the RNIB, Britain's biggest charity for the blind, was lukewarm. A spokesman said: 'We have a £2.5 million deficit and across the UK we believe that the lottery has affected us to the tune of £500,000.' By contrast, the Cancer Research Campaign was 'delighted' to receive £205,000 for a new breast cancer study in Glasgow. Another charity, Help the Aged was one of many whose application for Lottery funds was turned down at the first

By Dan Conaghan, Arts Correspondent

stage. A spokesman said: 'We are disappointed but we hope to receive something in the next two rounds.' The largest single grant, £660,000 went to the Strathclyde Poverty Alliance for projects to help the poor, and the smallest, £500, was for a toy library in Swindon.

The board's chief executive, Timothy Hornsby, defended a grant of more than £90,000 to the London-based Eritean Advice and Information Centre.

> ## 'Charities will always depend on the enormous generosity of the public and we urge everyone to continue'

'So much play has been made about one refugee group but it's a jolly good scheme,' he said. 'Less than one per cent is going to refugees. They need it. Less than three per cent is going to drug-related groups – and they need it.' The co-chairman of the advice centre, Tesfai Berhane, attended yesterdays announcement.

Mr Sieff said the list was 'tremendously exciting' for hundreds of charities throughout Britain: 'We said from the start we wanted to help small groups working at grass roots who don't often get a share of the big fund-raising money.'

He rejected claims that the board decided on the grants without public consultation, citing its survey

of nearly 8,000 charities. 'We held 25 seminars for some 5,000 people and as a result of that we came together to see what were the priorities. So you can hardly say we haven't consulted.'

The board's primary aim was to 'help those of greatest disadvantage in society and improve the quality of life in the community.'

There had been a big response from charities wanting money. Yesterday's list is the first of three in the next seven weeks totalling £162 million. 'That may seem a large amount but £162 million is only one per cent of the total income of the voluntary sector,' said Mr Sieff.

'Charities will always depend on the enormous generosity of the public and we urge everyone to continue.'

Smaller groups benefiting range from the Stanley Village playgroup in the East Midlands – £1,700 – to the London-based Vietnamese Mental Health Project, which receives £174,000.

The Yorkshire and Humberside-based Somali Mental Health Project, which tackles problems among refugees settled in Britain after fleeing the civil war in Somalia, was awarded £183,000.

Typical successful projects include victim-support groups, voluntary car schemes, swimming clubs for people with disabilities and help for people at risk of domestic violence.

The McCarthy Foundation, which helps elderly victims of violence and crime, said its grant of £183,000 had secured its future for three years.

Christine Bradley, the charity's administrator, said:

'We know our application met all the board's criteria but with so many people requesting funding we are extremely lucky. The grant application form looked horrific at first but it turned out to be straightforward and the application went smoothly.'

All those awarded grants yesterday can expect to be watched closely by the board to ensure the money is spent properly. Mr Hornsby said the grants would be 'tracked very carefully'. He added: 'No system can be 100 per cent flame-proof but we are satisfied we have put in place enough checks.'

Gratefully received – Highbury Nursery

'We need not worry about the boiler breaking down'

In recent years staff at the north London community nursery awaited winter with trepidation, writes Kathy Marks. The aged boiler that fires the heating system broke down regularly and children often had to keep on their coats and gloves. A £10,000 grant will be used to replace the boiler – a prosaic use of the money, but one that will ensure that the nursery's 30 children no longer have to run around just to keep warm. John Gilbert, the joint treasurer, said: 'We have just about managed to stay open in the past by importing electric heaters. This means that we no longer need worry about the boiler breaking

down so badly that we have to close.'

The independently-run nursery, in a Victorian terraced house, receives a £110,000 annual grant from Islington council and another £80,000 in means-tested parental contributions It caters for local children aged six months to five years, most of whose parents work full-time. Staff and parents had tried to raise money for a new boiler by holding car boot sales and charity dances but had made only relatively small headway. Mr Gilbert, who has two small children at the nursery, said: 'It was proving very difficult. Islington council are extremely supportive but they don't have the funds for major capital expenditure. The nursery is absolutely essential to the community. It provides a wonderful, loving atmosphere for our children.'

Gratefully received – Hartlepool CAB

'It's extremely good news for local residents'

Part of the bread-and-butter work of the busy Citizens' Advice Bureau in Hartlepool town centre is advising people in dispute with the Benefits Agency.

As funds are limited, however, some clients have to be turned away. A £52,000 grant will enable the

bureau to employ a case-worker for 30 hours a week for the next three years. The case-worker will provide representation for people at appeal tribunals whose benefit applications have been rejected; legal aid is not available in such cases.

Joe Michna, the CAB manager, said requests for such assistance had risen sharply over recent years. 'But people have virtually had to take pot luck as to whether we had someone available to help,' he said. 'We will now be able to provide a comprehensive and regular service. It is extremely good news for local residents.'

The bureau processes more than 13,000 enquiries a year on a core budget of £55,000 from the town council, Cleveland County Council and Hartlepool City Challenge. It employs three paid staff, helped by 24 volunteers.

Mr Michna said most disputes concerned such benefits as the Disability Living Allowance and the new Incapacity Benefit.

'Our new worker will provide moral support as well as help with the complex legal arguments. Many people are intimidated by the prospect of appearing before a tribunal.'

Beneficiaries

- Hundreds of small and large communities across the UK are benefiting from National Lottery funding

- £1,117 million raised for the Good Causes

- Total number of awards made: 1,432

- Awards under £25,000: 526 (36%)

- Awards under £100,000: 1,059 (74%)

- Awards under £1 million: 1,366 (95%)

- Awards over £1 million: 66 (5%)

Note: Figures up until 14 October 1995.
For a full list of grants contact:
National Lottery Division
Department of National Heritage
2/4 Cockspur Street
London, SW1Y 5DH
Tel: 0171 211 6200

- The above is an extract from *The National Lottery Fact File*, published by Camelot. See page 39 for address details.   © *Camelot*

Scratching out a living in a cold new world

After a year of the National Lottery, Janet Morrison assesses damage to the voluntary sector

By Janet Morrison

Where does the charity world stand at the end of the first full calendar year of the National Lottery? Several have experienced severe losses in their fundraising appeals. This could not come at a worse time for charities – whose sources of funding are under pressure.

Donations both from the public and from companies are static or falling and money from Government increasingly comes in the form of fees tied to providing services rather than grants. This means that charities cannot afford any further losses to their fundraising efforts. At the same time, many are on tenterhooks as to whether they can benefit from funds being given out by the five Lottery Distribution Boards.

The National Council for Voluntary Organisations (NCVO) has been measuring the effects of these developments. The results of opinion-polling show that fewer people are giving to charity. In July to September this year there were 10 per cent fewer people making donations than in the same period in 1992 and 1993. The estimated loss to charities in the first year could be as high as £339 million.

But who are the real losers? The Alexander Rose Day, which helps raise money for more than 1,000 charities through flag days and raffles, Actionaid through Actionaid week, and the National Schizophrenia Fellowship have all reported a dip in income.

It seems clear that people have less loose change to give because they are buying lottery tickets instead. This is borne out by the fact that it is street collections, door-to-door collections and small charity raffles and lotteries which are worst affected – the very activities that rely on a spontaneous reach into the pocket for small change.

Of course, not all charities are affected in the same way. Some have done better. In some cases, this is due to the use of more collectors or higher prizes in raffles; others have simply continued to build on traditionally loyal supporters. The one area of potential growth has been in charity scratch cards, which have benefited from lottery fever generated by Camelot's introduction of instant games in May.

UK Charity Lotteries, whose scratch card predates Camelot, have seen their takings increase fourfold in a matter of months. Scratch 'N' Win and Littlewoods games, which benefit named charities on their cards, have sprung up this year, and been very successful. Between them they have generated over £14 million for charity in just six months.

It is hard to assess what the long-term effects will be on charities' finances. NCVO is now jointly steering a Home Office research programme to examine charities' accounts to see the effects on their income. The results will be publicly available, but an interim report will not be available before next spring. The final report is not due till spring 1998.

Money has, of course, been coming back to the sector from the distribution boards which give out the National Lottery proceeds. Expectations, as well as applications, are high.

The National Lottery Charities Board – the only guaranteed source

of funds for fundraising charities – has been inundated by applications, receiving four times the number of the other four boards put together. Like the other boards, it gets only 5.6p in every £1 ticket sale. By the end of the year, they will have given out over £240 million to specific charities.

The first round of grants went to poverty projects. With concerns about the social effects of the Lottery high, this theme struck a welcome note in the voluntary sector. The grants made so far have gone to a wide range of projects – in terms of activity, size and geography.

Some commentators have called for grant-giving to be a beauty contest favouring the causes already popular with the public. However, NCVO believes that Lottery money should not just go to the popular causes but should benefit all parts of the community, and should pay for new projects as well as those tried and tested by the established 'big name' charities.

The NLCB has made a good start to a difficult job and has proved itself independent of political influence.

> ### By the end of the year The National Lottery Charities Board will have given out over £240 million to specific charities

There is still more that could be done to help charities. NCVO will continue to urge a serious review of the share-out between the five boards – sports, arts, millennium, national heritage and charities. In view of the losses to fundraising charities and the demand for grants, NCVO believes there is a strong case for the Government to look at ways of increasing the 5.6 per cent share currently available to the NLCB. The overall losses to charity fundraising, and the high level of demand for grants, show that this is appropriate. In this, we are supported by the general public. A recent MORI poll in the *Daily Express* shows that the public want 32p in the pound to go to charity.

At the same time, a beady eye needs to be directed at the Government's 12 per cent tax take. This is higher than nearly every other country. In Italy, the Netherlands and Portugal tax is levied on prizes rather than the whole turnover. There is no reason why the same could not be done here to benefit the amount available to good causes.

One of the most vexed questions will be how distribution of grants affects existing government responsibilities and funding. There is real concern that the existence of Lottery money might encourage funders to make cuts in their grants, or otherwise substitute for activities formerly the function of the state.

This will be harder to measure – particularly since the role and responsibilities of the state are ever-shifting and nowhere defined. NCVO and others, no doubt, will need to address this issue in more detail very soon.

● Janet Morrison is director of policy at the National Council for Voluntary Organisations.   *© The Guardian December, 1995*

Problem gambling

From the Scottish Office

Gambling can be addictive or compulsive to some individuals and it can cause others financial and other problems even if they are not addicted. The American Psychiatric Association has defined the essential features of compulsive gambling as 'a continuous or periodic loss of control over gambling; a progression, in frequency and amount wagered, in the preoccupation with gambling and in obtaining monies to gamble; and a continuation of the behaviour despite adverse consequences'.

Problem gambling covers a wider group including those with lesser or occasional difficulties with their gambling behaviour. To a large degree, the extent, and potential adverse consequences, of problem gambling have been controlled in this country by the restrictive regime applied to gambling generally and to gaming in particular. Of especial relevance to this have been the principle that facilities should be no more than adequate to meet the unstimulated demand for them and the controls on advertising and promotion, on access to gambling facilities and on gambling on credit.

There is generally agreed to be a correlation between the amount of problem gambling and addiction and the availability and accessibility of gambling outlets. There are reports that the widespread availability of the National Lottery is having an impact and the advent of Sunday racing and betting will provide further opportunities to gamble. The Board believes that there should be research into and monitoring of the impact of such increased opportunities, by both the authorities and the industry. There is something of a lack of research generally into problem gambling in Great Britain. In this respect, the Board has welcomed two recent studies commissioned by the Home Office and the British Casino Association into the issues in general. In a separate development, the Board has also welcomed the proposal by a number of casino and other gaming operators to establish and support a Chair of Gambling Studies at the University of Salford.

● The above is an extract from the *Report of the Gaming Board for Great Britain 1994/95*, published by the Home Office, Scottish Office.
© Home Office, Scottish Office January, 1996

INDEX

ADDITIONAL RESOURCES

You might like to contact the following organisations for further information. Due to the increasing cost of postage, many organisations cannot respond to enquiries unless they receive a stamped, addressed envelope.

Bingo Association of Great Britain
BAGB Press Office
Attenborough Associates
Waverley House
7-2 Noel Street
London, W1V 4NN
Tel: 0171 734 4455
The trade association for the amusement machine industry in Great Britain. Produces publications.

BACTA
BACTA House
Regents Wharf
6 All Saints Street
London
N12 9QR
Tel: 0171 713 7144
Fax: 0171 713 0446
BACTA is the trade association for the amusement machine industry in Great Britain. Produces publications.

British Casino Association
29 Castle Street
Reading
Berkshire, RG1 7SL
Tel: 01734 589 191
Fax: 01734 590 592
The trade association for the Casino industry in Great Britain. Produces publications.

Camelot plc
Public Affairs Department
Tolpits Lane
Watford, WD1 8RN
Tel: 01923 425000
Fax: 01923 425050
Organisers of the National Lottery. They produce a fact pack, an annual report and other useful information. Available from the Public Affairs Department.

Council of Churches for Britain and Ireland (CCBI)
Interchurch House
35 - 41 Lower Marsh
London, SE1 7RC
Tel: 0171 620 4444

Gamblers Anonymous and Gam-Anon
PO Box 88
London, SW6 3EU
Tel: 0171 384 3040 (National helpline)
Gamblers Anonymous is a self-help fellowship of men and women who have joined together to do something about their gambling problem, and carry the message to help others. Produces publications.

Gaming Board for Great Britain
Lotteries Section
Berkshire House
168-173 High Holborn
London, WC1A 7AA
Tel: 0171 306 6200
Fax: 0171 306 6266
Produces an annual report on the gaming industry.

Gordon House Association
186 Mackenzie Road
Beckenham
Kent, BR3 4SF
Tel: 0181 778 3331
A 13 bed unit with a national catchment area providing a therapeutic residential environment and both group and individual counselling for residents whilst at the hostel and after their planned return to the community.

National Council for Social Concern
59 Catherine Place
London, SW1E 6DY
Tel: 0171 630 7046
Fax: 0171 630 9814
Promotes the restoration of the community of ex-offenders and of people addicted to alcohol, drugs or gambling. Produces an information pack for students and other publications.

National Council on Gambling
7 Longleat Road
Bush Hill Park
Enfield
Middlesex

EN1 2QJ
Tel: 0181 364 1376
Fax: 0181 364 1376
Works to advance public education about the incidence and effect on society of gambling in all its forms.

National Lottery Charities Board
7th Floor
St Vincent House
30 Orange Street
London, WC2H 7HH
Tel: 0171 747 5300
Fax: 0171 747 5214
The National Lotteries Charities Board can make grants to charitable, benevolent or philanthropic organisations.

Office of the National Lottery (OFLOT)
2 Monck Street
London, SW1P 2BQ
Tel: 0345 125596
A non-ministerial government department which regulates the National Lottery. They produce a wide range of information leaflets and background notes.

UK Charity Lotteries (UCKL)
Buttermere House
Western Avenue Office Centre
Kendal Avenue
London, W3 0XA
Tel: 0181 992 8800
Fax: 0181 992 4642

UK Forum on Young People and Gambling
PO Box 5
Chicester
West Sussex, PO19 3RB
Tel: 01243 538 635
Promotes public education and training on young people and gambling (now including electronic game playing). In addition to running training courses and workshops, they produce a newsletter, a wide range of useful leaflets and other publications.

ACKNOWLEDGEMENTS

The publisher is grateful for permission to reproduce the following material.

Chapter One: The Issues

Spotlight on gambling, © The National Council for Social Concern, *UK Forum on Young People and Gambling*, © UK Forum on Young People and Gambling, *Lottomania!*, © More! Magazine, August, 1995, *Adolescent gambling*, © Routledge, *The National Lottery and scratch cards*, © Gamblers Anonymous, November 1995, *Gambling with their childhood*, © The Guardian, October 1995, *Teenagers who forget age limits for an instant*, © The Independent, November 1995, *How to spot child gamblers*, © The Daily Mirror, November 1995, *Young gambling*, © UK Forum on Young People and Gambling, *ID cards call for teenage gamblers*, © The Independent, January 1996, *Age limits for gambling*, © Home Office, *My guilty secret . . .I'm hooked on the National Lottery*, © Just Seventeen, *Scratch cards and lottery tickets*, © The Guardian, July 1995, *The thrill is not the kill*, © The Independent, January 1996, *Gambling with the nation's health?*, © British Medical Journal, August 1995, *Lotteryisms win instant acceptance*, © The Independent, December 1995, *Help is at hand*, © Gamblers Anonymous, *Hope for compulsive gamblers*, © Gordon House Association, *Lottery jackpot curb is rejected*, © The Telegraph plc, London 1995, *The British Amusement industry*, © The British Amusement, Catering Trade Association (BACTA), *The casino industry*, © British Casino Association, *Bingo and Gaming*, © The Bingo Association of Great Britain.

Chapter Two: Funding

A guide to the National Lottery, © The Office of the National Lottery (OFLOT), 1995, *Profile of players*, © Camelot, *Winning projects for the people in need*, © The Guardian, October 1995, *It could be your good cause*, © HMSO Reproduced with the kind permission of Her Majesty's Stationery Office, 1995, *Worldwide lottery facts*, © Camelot. *Lottery refuses 9 in 10 charities*, © The Guardian , October 1995, *A nation of winners*, Reproduction of the 'Camelot' logo and the extract from the 1995 annual report is made with the permission of of Camelot Group plc, *Allocation of funds*, © Camelot, *Council of Churches for Britain and Ireland (CCBI)*, © The Council of Churches for Britain and Ireland, November 1995, *Churches attack big-win lottery but take the cash*, © The Telegraph plc, London 1995, *Where £40 million handout is going*, © The Telegraph plc, London 1995, *Beneficiaries*, © Camelot, *Scratching out a living in a cold new world*, © The Guardian, December 1995.

Photographs and Illustrations

Pages 1, 7, 30: Anthony Haythornthwaite / Folio Collective, pages 3, 14, 18: Andrew Smith / Folio Collective, pages 8, 11: Katherine Fleming / Folio Collective, pages 12, 36: Ken Pyne, pages 19, 27, 32: Graphic News, pages 26, 31: Reproducion of the 'Camelot' logo is made with the permission of Camelot Group plc.

Craig Donnellan
Cambridge
April, 1996